Texas
GoMath!

Volume 2

Houghton
Mifflin
Harcourt

© Houghton Mifflin Harcourt Publishing Company • Image Credits: © Fuse/Getty Images

Texas
GoMath!

ISBN 978-0-544-08676-0

13 0928 22 21

4500820950   B C D E F G

Cover Image Credits: (longhorn) ©Fuse/Getty Images; (mountains) ©B. Franklin/Shutterstock; (lizard) ©Matt Jeppson/Shutterstock; (bridge) ©David Sucsy/Getty Images.

Dear Students and Families,

Welcome to **Texas Go Math!**, Grade 1! In this exciting mathematics program, there are hands-on activities to do and real-world problems to solve. Best of all, you will write your ideas and answers right in your book. In **Texas Go Math!**, writing and drawing on the pages helps you think deeply about what you are learning, and you will really understand math!

By the way, all of the pages in your **Texas Go Math!** book are made using recycled paper. We wanted you to know that you can Go Green with **Texas Go Math!**

Sincerely,

The Authors

Made in the United States
Printed on 100% recycled paper

Texas
*Go*Math!

Authors

Juli K. Dixon, Ph.D.
Professor, Mathematics
    Education
University of Central Florida
Orlando, Florida

Edward B. Burger, Ph.D.
President
Southwestern University
Georgetown, Texas

Matthew R. Larson, Ph.D.
K-12 Curriculum Specialist for
    Mathematics
Lincoln Public Schools
Lincoln, Nebraska

Martha E. Sandoval-Martinez
Math Instructor
El Camino College
Torrance, California

Consultant

Valerie Johse
Math Consultant
Texas Council for Economic
    Education
Houston, Texas

Volume 1

Unit 1 • Number and Operations: Place Value, Addition and Subtraction Concepts

Look for these:

H.O.T. Problems
Higher Order Thinking
Multi-Step Problems

Module 1 • Number Sense – Tens and Ones

Homework and Practice

Homework and TEKS Practice in every lesson.

Module 2 • Compare Numbers

Module 3 • Add Tens and Ones

GO DIGITAL Resources

DIGITAL RESOURCES
Go online for the Interactive Student Edition with Math on the Spot Videos. Use *i*Tools, the Multimedia *e*Glossary, and more.

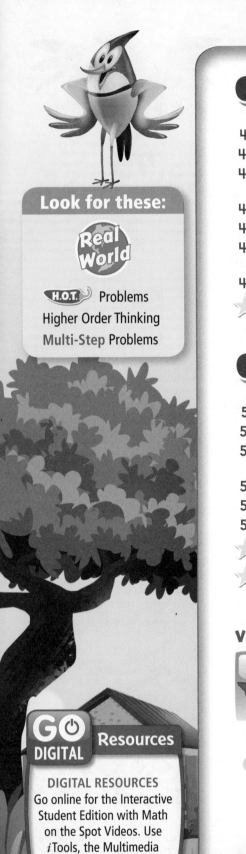

Module 4 — Addition Concepts

Module 5 — Subtraction Concepts

Volume 1

Unit 2 • Number and Operations: Addition and Subtraction Strategies, Money

Module 6 • Addition Strategies

Module 7 • Subtraction Strategies

Module 8 • Addition and Subtraction Word Problems

Module 9 • Money

Look for these:

Real World

H.O.T. Problems
Higher Order Thinking
Multi-Step Problems

Homework and Practice

Homework and TEKS Practice in every lesson.

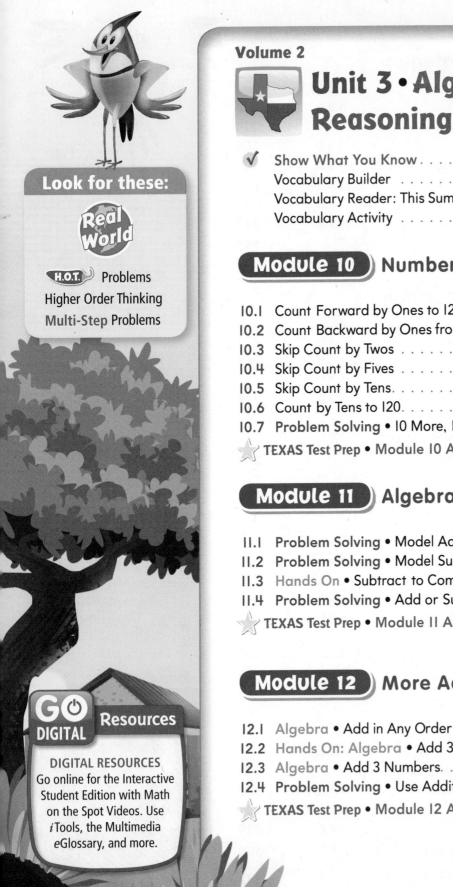

Volume 2

Unit 3 • Algebraic Reasoning

Module 10 — Number Patterns to 120

Module 11 — Algebraic Reasoning

Module 12 — More Addition Strategies

Look for these:

Real World

H.O.T. Problems
Higher Order Thinking
Multi-Step Problems

GO DIGITAL Resources

DIGITAL RESOURCES
Go online for the Interactive
Student Edition with Math
on the Spot Videos. Use
*i*Tools, the Multimedia
eGlossary, and more.

Module 13 • Addition and Subtraction Relationships

Look for these:

H.O.T. Problems
Higher Order Thinking
Multi-Step Problems

Volume 2

Unit 4 • Geometry and Measurement

Homework and Practice

Homework and TEKS Practice in every lesson.

Module 14 • Geometry: Two-Dimensional Shapes

Look for these:

Real World

H.O.T. Problems
Higher Order Thinking
Multi-Step Problems

Module 15) Geometry: Three-Dimensional Solids

Module 16) Fraction Concepts

Module 17) Measurement

GO DIGITAL Resources

DIGITAL RESOURCES
Go online for the Interactive
Student Edition with Math
on the Spot Videos. Use
*i*Tools, the Multimedia
*e*Glossary, and more.

Module 18 · Time

Volume 2

Unit 5 · Data Analysis

Module 19 · Graphing

Look for these:

H.O.T. Problems
Higher Order Thinking
Multi-Step Problems

Homework and TEKS Practice in every lesson.

Look for these:

Real World

H.O.T. Problems
Higher Order Thinking
Multi-Step Problems

GO DIGITAL Resources

DIGITAL RESOURCES
Go online for the Interactive Student Edition with Math on the Spot Videos. Use *i*Tools, the Multimedia *e*Glossary, and more.

Algebraic Reasoning

© Houghton Mifflin Harcourt Publishing Company

Show What You Know ✓

Check your understanding of important skills.

Name _____

Model More, Model Fewer

1. Circle the row that has more.

2. Circle the row that has fewer.

Count On

Use the number line to add. Write each sum.

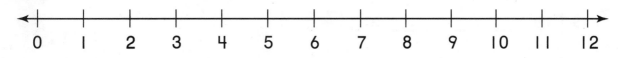

3. 6 + 3 = ___ | 4. 7 + 1 = ___ | 5. 8 + 2 = ___

Count Back

Use the number line to subtract. Write each difference.

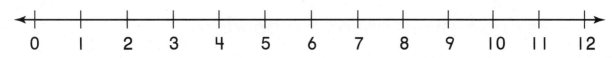

6. 11 − 2 = ___ | 7. 8 − 3 = ___ | 8. 9 − 1 = ___

FAMILY NOTE: This page checks your child's understanding of important skills needed for success in Unit 3.

 GO DIGITAL Assessment Options: **Soar to Success Math**

Vocabulary Builder

Review Words

add
difference
fewer
more
same
subtract
sum

Visualize It

Sort the review words from the box.

Addition Words   **Subtraction Words**

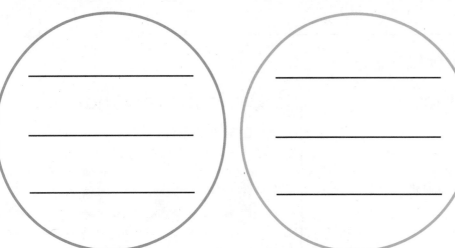

_____   _____

_____   _____

_____   _____

Understand Vocabulary

Use a review word to complete each sentence.

1. 8 is the _____ for 17 − 9.

2. 17 is the _____ for 8 + 9.

3. When you _____ 4 to 8,
   you find the sum.

4. 5 ducks and 5 swans are at the pond.

   There are the _____ number
   of ducks and swans.

GO DIGITAL • Interactive Student Edition
                • Multimedia eGlossary

This Summer I Wish I Could . . .

written by Chloe Weasley

illustrated by Claudine Gevry

This Take-Home Book belongs to

_____

Reading and Writing Math

This take-home book will help you recognize addition and subtraction situations.

MATHEMATICAL PROCESSES 1.1.A, 1.1.D

To my surprise and great delight
Our teacher asked us to draw or write
About something we would think so cool
To do this summer when out of school.
So many ideas swirled in my head!
"There are lots of things I'd do," I said.

354

I'd sail the ocean in a boat.
My first mate would be a goat.
From the starboard side we'd see
A pod of whales. There would be 3.
Then I'd spy 4 whales more!
Oh, such a summer I'd adore.

How many whales do they see in all?

_____ + _____ = _____ whales

I'd take a rocket to where it's starry.
Oh, what fun, an outer space safari!
The first of many stops would be
Our moon, where moon mountains
I would see.

356

How many moon mountains are tall?
How many are short?
How many moon mountains are there
in all?

_____ + _____ = _____ moon mountains

Or perhaps this summer time,
My goat and I would take a climb.
Then build a house up in a tree.
A farm and far off city we could see.
How many cows? How many horses?
How many fewer horses than cows?

_____ – _____ = _____ fewer horses

But really and truly the most fun
Is when in summer I play and run,
Or read a book beneath a tree
And simply watch a bumble bee.

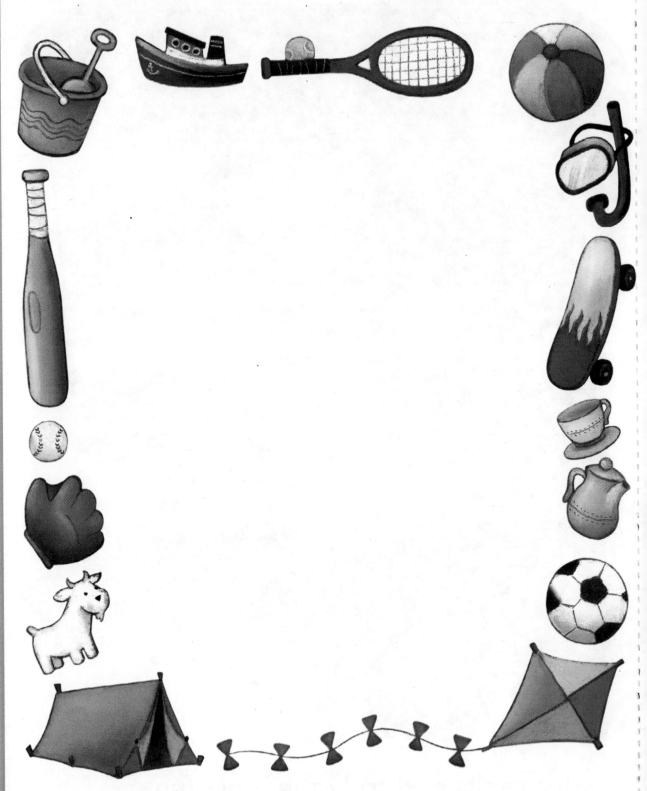

Now it's your turn to write or draw.
Think of summer and what you'd do,
If you could plan what's best for you!

Name _____

Write Math ▸ Look at the pictures. Draw and write your own story about the whales. Use addition and subtraction in your story.

Vocabulary Review
addition
fewer
more
subtraction

_____
_ _
_____

_____
_ _
_____

_____
_ _
_____

More and Fewer

Look at the picture. Complete the number sentences.

1. How many cows and horses are there?

   _____ + _____ = _____

2. How many more cows are there than horses?

   _____ − _____ = _____ more cows

3. Four cows go into the barn.
   How many cows are there now?

   _____ − _____ = _____ cows

MATH BOARD   Write a story problem about animals you see on a farm. Use the words more or fewer in your story. Have a classmate solve the problem.

_____

_____

_____

TEKS Algebraic
Reasoning—1.5.A
MATHEMATICAL PROCESSES
1.1.D, 1.1.F, 1.1.G

10.1 Count Forward by Ones to 120

? Essential Question

How can knowing a counting pattern help you count to 120?

Explore

Write the numbers as you count forward.

21	22	23	24	25	26	27	28	29	30
31	32	33	34	35	36	37	38	39	40
41	42	43	44	45	46	47	48	49	50
51	52	53	54	55	56	57	58	59	60
61	62	63	64	65	66	67	68	69	70
71	72	73	74	75	76	77	78	79	80
81	82	83	84	85	86	87	88	89	90
91	92	93	94	95	96	97	98	99	100

 FOR THE TEACHER • Read the following problem. Debbie saw this page in a puzzle book. Two rows of numbers are incomplete. Use what you know about counting forward to write the numbers.

Math Talk
Mathematical Processes

Explain how you know which numbers to write.

Count forward.
Write the numbers.

1	2	3	4	5	6	7	8	9	10
11	12	13	14	15	16	17	18	19	20
21	22	23	24	25	26	27	28	29	30
31	32	33	34	35	36	37	38	39	40
41	42	43	44	45	46	47	48	49	50
51	52	53	54	55	56	57	58	59	60
61	62	63	64	65	66	67	68	69	70
71	72	73	74	75	76	77	78	79	80
81	82	83	84	85	86	87	88	89	90
91	92	93	94	95	96	97	98	99	100
101	102	103	104	105	106	107	108	109	110
111	112	113	114	115	116	117	118	119	120

10, __11__, _____, _____, _____

100, __101__, _____, _____, _____

110, __111__, _____, _____, _____

Share and Show   MATH BOARD

Use a Counting Chart. Count forward.
Write the numbers.

> Look for a pattern to help you write the numbers.

1. 114, _____, _____, _____, _____, _____, _____

2. 51, _____, _____, _____, _____, _____, _____

3. 94, _____, _____, _____, _____, _____, _____

4. 78, _____, _____, _____, _____, _____, _____

☑5. 35, _____, _____, _____, _____, _____, _____

☑6. 104, _____, _____, _____, _____, _____, _____

Name _____

Use a Counting Chart. Count forward.
Write the numbers.

7. 19, _____, _____, _____, _____, _____, _____, _____, _____

8. 98, _____, _____, _____, _____, _____, _____, _____, _____

9. 107, _____, _____, _____, _____, _____, _____, _____, _____

10. 43, _____, _____, _____, _____, _____, _____, _____, _____

11. 68, _____, _____, _____, _____, _____, _____, _____, _____

12. 50, _____, _____, _____, _____, _____, _____, _____, _____

13. **H.O.T.** Use a Counting Chart to write the numbers counting forward.

_____, _____, _____, _____, _____, 120

14. **H.O.T.** **Multi-Step** There is an unknown number in the sequence counting forward. The number is greater than 51. The number is less than 53. What is the unknown number? _____

Choose the correct answer.

15. Count forward. Which numbers come next?

115, 116, _____, _____, _____, _____

○ 17, 18, 19, 20
○ 117, 118, 119, 120
○ 7, 8, 9, 10

16. A jar has 97 marbles in it. There are 3 marbles on the table. Count forward as you put each marble in the jar. How many marbles are in the jar?

○ 100   ○ 99   ○ 93

17. **Display** Some of the numbers are not shown. Count forward. Write the numbers that are not shown.

| 31 | 32 | 33 | 34 | | |

18. ⭐ **TEXAS Test Prep** Count forward. What number is not shown?

107, 108, 109, _____, 111

○ 100   ○ 110   ○ 101

TAKE HOME ACTIVITY • Take a walk with your child. Count aloud together as you take 120 steps.

10.1 Count Forward by Ones to 120

Use a Counting Chart. Count forward. Write the numbers.

1	2	3	4	5	6	7	8	9	10
11	12	13	14	15	16	17	18	19	20
21	22	23	24	25	26	27	28	29	30
31	32	33	34	35	36	37	38	39	40
41	42	43	44	45	46	47	48	49	50
51	52	53	54	55	56	57	58	59	60
61	62	63	64	65	66	67	68	69	70
71	72	73	74	75	76	77	78	79	80
81	82	83	84	85	86	87	88	89	90
91	92	93	94	95	96	97	98	99	100
101	102	103	104	105	106	107	108	109	110
111	112	113	114	115	116	117	118	119	120

1. 62, _____, _____, _____

2. 21, _____, _____, _____

3. 104, _____, _____, _____, _____, _____

4. 48, _____, _____, _____, _____, _____, _____

Problem Solving Real World

Use a Counting Chart.

5. Jill has a set of number cards. Some of the cards are missing. Count forward. Fill in the numbers of the missing cards.

___29___ , _____, _____, ___32___, _____, ___34___

Choose the correct answer.

6. Count forward. Which numbers come next?

98, 99, _____, _____, _____, _____

○ 94, 95, 96, 97
○ 0, 1, 2, 3
○ 100, 101, 102, 103

7. Sally counted the shells in her collection.
Count forward. Which numbers are not shown?

71	72		74		76

○ 72 and 74   ○ 73 and 75   ○ 72 and 76

8. **Multi-Step** There are 58 books in the
bookcase. There are 2 books on the table
and 2 on the chair. Count forward as you
put each book in the bookcase. How
many books are in the bookcase?

○ 62   ○ 54   ○ 60

9. Count forward.
What number is not shown? 97, 98, 99, _____, 101

○ 90   ○ 100   ○ 101

TEKS Algebraic Reasoning—1.5.A

MATHEMATICAL PROCESSES
1.1.D, 1.1.F, 1.1.G

10.2 Count Backward by Ones from 120

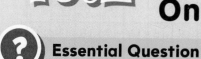

? **Essential Question**

How can knowing a counting pattern help you count backward from 120?

Explore Real World

Count backward from 30. Write the numbers as you count backward.

									10
11	12	13	14	15	16	17	18	19	20
21	22	23	24	25	26	27	28	29	30
31	32	33	34	35	36	37	38	39	40
41	42	43	44	45	46	47	48	49	50
51	52	53	54	55	56	57	58	59	60
61	62	63	64	65	66	67	68	69	70
71	72	73	74	75	76	77	78	79	80
81	82	83	84	85	86	87	88	89	90
91	92	93	94	95	96	97	98	99	100

FOR THE TEACHER • Read the following problem. Miss Simmons is checking off the children as they leave the room. One row of numbers is incomplete. Use what you know about counting backward to write the numbers.

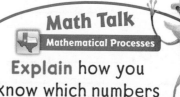

Math Talk
Mathematical Processes

Explain how you know which numbers to write.

Model and Draw

Count backward.
Write the numbers.

1	2	3	4	5	6	7	8	9	10
11	12	13	14	15	16	17	18	19	20
21	22	23	24	25	26	27	28	29	30
31	32	33	34	35	36	37	38	39	40
41	42	43	44	45	46	47	48	49	50
51	52	53	54	55	56	57	58	59	60
61	62	63	64	65	66	67	68	69	70
71	72	73	74	75	76	77	78	79	80
81	82	83	84	85	86	87	88	89	90
91	92	93	94	95	96	97	98	99	100
101	102	103	104	105	106	107	108	109	110
111	112	113	114	115	116	117	118	119	120

10, _9_ , _____ , _____ , _____

100, _99_ , _____ , _____ , _____

110, _109_ , _____ , _____ , _____

Share and Show

Use a Counting Chart. Count backward. Write the numbers.

Look for a pattern to help you write the numbers.

1. 114, _____ , _____ , _____ , _____ , _____ , _____

2. 51, _____ , _____ , _____ , _____ , _____ , _____

3. 94, _____ , _____ , _____ , _____ , _____ , _____

4. 78, _____ , _____ , _____ , _____ , _____ , _____

☑5. 35, _____ , _____ , _____ , _____ , _____ , _____

☑6. 109, _____ , _____ , _____ , _____ , _____ , _____

Problem Solving

Use a Counting Chart. Count backward.
Write the numbers.

7. 19, ____, ____, ____, ____, ____, ____, ____, ____

8. 86, ____, ____, ____, ____, ____, ____, ____, ____

9. 107, ____, ____, ____, ____, ____, ____, ____, ____

10. 43, ____, ____, ____, ____, ____, ____, ____, ____

11. 68, ____, ____, ____, ____, ____, ____, ____, ____

12. 22, ____, ____, ____, ____, ____, ____, ____, ____

13. **H.O.T.** Use a Counting Chart to write the numbers counting backward.

120, ____, ____, ____, ____, ____

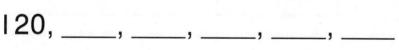

14. **H.O.T.** **Multi-Step** There is an unknown number in the sequence counting backward. The number is after 48. The number is before 46. What is the unknown number? ____

Mathematical Processes
Model • Reason • Communicate

Choose the correct answer.

15. **Analyze** Shawn is counting backward from 101. He is stuck at 100. Which numbers come next?

101, 100, _____, _____, _____, _____

- ○ 95, 90, 85, 80
- ○ 90, 80, 70, 60
- ○ 99, 98, 97, 96

16. Jackie has 25 toy cars. Each car has a number on it from 1 to 25. Jackie wants to put the cars in order from the greatest number to the least. She finds the first three cars. Which car number comes next?

- ○ 20
- ○ 22
- ○ 15

17. Dan left a number off the chart. Write the number that is not shown.

120	119	118	117		115	114	113	112	111

18. ⭐ **TEXAS Test Prep** Count backward. What number is not shown?

120, 119, _____, 117, 116

- ○ 118
- ○ 117
- ○ 120

TAKE HOME ACTIVITY • Place 10 objects in a row. Have your child point to each object as he or she counts backward from 10.

Homework and Practice

Name _____

10.2 Count Backward by Ones to 120

Use a Counting Chart. Count backward. Write the numbers.

1	2	3	4	5	6	7	8	9	10
11	12	13	14	15	16	17	18	19	20
21	22	23	24	25	26	27	28	29	30
31	32	33	34	35	36	37	38	39	40
41	42	43	44	45	46	47	48	49	50
51	52	53	54	55	56	57	58	59	60
61	62	63	64	65	66	67	68	69	70
71	72	73	74	75	76	77	78	79	80
81	82	83	84	85	86	87	88	89	90
91	92	93	94	95	96	97	98	99	100
101	102	103	104	105	106	107	108	109	110
111	112	113	114	115	116	117	118	119	120

1. 41, _____, _____, _____

2. 83, _____, _____, _____

3. 104, _____, _____, _____, _____, _____

4. 30, _____, _____, _____, _____, _____, _____

Problem Solving Real World

Use a Counting Chart.

5. Jed has a book with missing pages. Count backward. Fill in the numbers of the missing pages.

_____, 24 , 23 , _____, _____, 20 , _____, _____

Lesson Check

Choose the correct answer.

6 Andy is learning to count backward.
His teacher left some numbers off the chart.
Which numbers are not shown?

83	82	81		79	78		76	75

○ 79 and 82   ○ 70 and 75   ○ 80 and 77

7. Cal and Kim are counting backward from 43.
They don't agree over which numbers
come next. Which numbers are correct?

43, 42, _____, _____, _____, _____

○ 41, 40, 39, 38
○ 43, 44, 45, 46
○ 40, 30, 20, 10

8. Multi-Step Jack counted the stamps
in his collection. The number of stamps is
more than 61. The number is less than 63.
How many stamps does he have?

○ 67   ○ 62   ○ 60

9. Count backward.
What number is not shown? 82, 81, 80, _____, 78, 77

○ 81   ○ 76   ○ 79

TEKS Algebraic Reasoning—1.5.B
MATHEMATICAL PROCESSES
1.1.C, 1.1.F, 1.1.G

10.3 Skip Count by Twos

 Essential Question How can skip counting by twos help to count objects in a set?

Explore

Place as shown. Skip count by twos.
Write to show how many.

2

4

6

_____

_____

_____

Math Talk
Mathematical Processes

Explain How does skip counting by twos help you count sets of objects?

FOR THE TEACHER • Read the following problem. Skylar has 12 socks. How can skip counting by twos help her to count the socks?

Model and Draw

Skip count the acorns by twos to find how many.

How many are you counting each time?

___ ___ ___ ___ ___

___ ___ ___ ___ ___

Share and Show

MATH BOARD

Skip count. Count the shoes by twos. Write how many.

THINK
What is the best way to count these objects?

✓ I.

___ ___ ___ ___ ___

___ ___ ___ ___ ___

Name _____

Skip count. Write how many.

2.

_____ pennies

3.

_____ shells

Use skip counting by twos to solve.
Write or draw to explain.

Math on the Spot

4. **H.O.T.** There are two colors on each paint tray. How many colors would be on 50 trays?

_____ colors

5. **H.O.T.** **Multi-Step** There are 30 children in the class. Each child has a bicycle. There are two tires on each bicycle. How many tires are there?

_____ tires

Choose the correct answer.

6. There are 70 dancers on the dance floor.
Skip count. How many groups of 2 are
on the floor?

○ 25   ○ 35   ○ 22

7. **Display** Alyssa is placing socks in pairs.
Skip count by twos.
Which numbers come next?

102, 104, _____, _____, _____

○ 6, 8, 10
○ 105, 106, 107
○ 106, 108, 110

8. Kenny is using a hundred chart to count
his pennies. He places a penny on every
other number in the chart. He skip
counts by twos to count his pennies.
Write how many pennies Kenny uses.   _____

9. ⭐ **TEXAS Test Prep** Which number comes after
114 when skip counting by twos?

○ 16   ○ 116   ○ 115

TAKE HOME ACTIVITY • Give your child a handful of pennies. Have
him or her group the pennies in pairs, and then count them by twos.

TEKS Algebraic Reasoning—1.5.B
MATHEMATICAL PROCESSES 1.1.C, 1.1.F, 1.1.G

Name _____

10.3 Skip Count by Twos

Skip count. Count the cherries by twos.
Write how many.

1.

___ ___ ___ ___ ___ ___

2. Skip count. Write how many.

____ socks

Problem Solving Real World

Use skip counting by twos to solve.
Write or draw to explain.

3. There are 2 pictures on every page
of a book. There are 13 pages in the
book. How many pictures are in
the book?

____ pictures

Choose the correct answer.

4. There are 60 twins in the town. Skip count. How many pairs of twins are in the town?

○ 20   ○ 63   ○ 30

5. **Multi-Step** Carla has 5 flower pots. She plants 2 seeds in each pot. Then she plants 2 more seeds in each pot. Skip count by twos. How many seeds did Carla plant?

○ 9   ○ 20   ○ 10

6. Which number comes after 58 when skip counting by twos?

○ 50   ○ 59   ○ 60

7. Georgia is counting footprints at the beach. Skip count by twos. Write the numbers that come next.

22, 24, _____, _____, _____, _____

TEKS Algebraic
Reasoning—1.5.B
MATHEMATICAL PROCESSES
1.1.C, 1.1.F, 1.1.G

10.4 Skip Count by Fives

 Essential Question

How can skip counting by fives help to count objects in a set?

Explore

Skip count by fives. Write to show how many fingers.

_____   _____   _____   _____   _____

_____   _____   _____   _____   _____

Math Talk
Mathematical Processes

Explain When is it easier to count a set of objects by fives?

 FOR THE TEACHER • Read the following problem. How many hands would it take to show 50 fingers?

Model and Draw

How many are you counting each time?

Skip count the candles by fives to find how many.

_____ _____ _____ _____ _____ _____

_____ _____ _____ _____ _____ _____

Share and Show

 MATH BOARD

THINK
What is the best way to count these objects?

Skip count. Count the petals on the flowers by fives. Write how many.

1.

_____ _____ _____ _____ _____

_____ _____ _____ _____ _____

_____ _____ _____ _____ _____

_____ _____ _____ _____ _____

382 three hundred eighty-two

Name _____

Skip count. Write how many.

2.

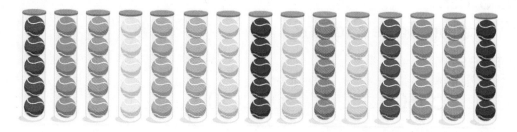

_____ balls

3.

_____ points

Use skip counting by fives to solve.
Write or draw to explain.

4. **H.O.T.** There are five arms
on each starfish. How many
arms are on 22 starfish?

_____ arms

5. **H.O.T.** **Multi-Step** Emma saves
5 cents a day. How many cents
does she have in one week?

_____ cents

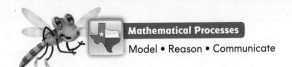

Mathematical Processes
Model • Reason • Communicate

Choose the correct answer.

6. **Analyze** Jake's farm has 10 ponds.
Each pond has 5 fish.
How many fish are on Jake's farm?
Skip count by fives.

○ 20   ○ 50   ○ 100

7. Gary likes to count his puzzle pieces by
fives. Which numbers complete the skip
count by fives sequence?

95, _____, 105, 110, _____

○ 100 and 115   ○ 96 and 111   ○ 100 and 111

8. **Multi-Step** Jenna collects baseball cards.
She groups them in fives, and puts 2 groups
in 1 stack. Jenna has 10 stacks of cards.
How many cards does Jenna have?

○ 50   ○ 100   ○ 25

9. ⭐ **TEXAS Test Prep** Which number comes after
95 when skip counting by fives?

○ 96   ○ 105   ○ 100

TAKE HOME ACTIVITY • Have your child use buttons or beans to make
groups of five. Then have him or her count by fives to tell how many objects.

TEKS Algebraic Reasoning—1.5.B
MATHEMATICAL PROCESSES 1.1.C, 1.1.F, 1.1.G

Name _____

10.4 Skip Count by Fives

Skip count. Count the fish in the bowls by fives. Write how many.

1.

_____ _____ _____ _____ _____ _____

_____ _____ _____ _____ _____ _____

_____ _____ _____ _____ _____ _____

Problem Solving Real World

Use skip counting by fives to solve.
Write or draw to explain.

2. Chet counts balloons for a party. He counts 13 bunches of balloons. Each bunch has 5 balloons. How many balloons does Chet count?

_____ balloons

Choose the correct answer.

3. Willy makes groups of 5 to count his crayons. He makes 9 groups. How many crayons does Willy have?

○ 90   ○ 45   ○ 18

4. Count by fives. Which numbers are not shown?

90, 95, _____, 105, _____, 115

○ 96 and 106

○ 100 and 106

○ 100 and 110

5. **Multi-Step** There are 5 chickens in each pen. There are 4 pens in the barn. There are 2 pens outside. How many chickens are there?

○ 30   ○ 40   ○ 20

6. Write the number that comes after 100 when skip counting by fives.

_____

Name _____

10.5 Skip Count by Tens

 Essential Question How can skip counting by tens help to count objects in a set?

Explore

Skip count by tens. Write to show how many crayons.

_____10_____   _____   _____   _____

_____   _____   _____   _____

_____   _____   _____   _____

 FOR THE TEACHER • Read the following problem. How many crayons would there be in 12 groups of 10 crayons?

Math Talk
Mathematical Processes

Explain When would it be useful to count by tens?

© Houghton Mifflin Harcourt Publishing Company

Skip count the toes by tens to find how many.

How many are you counting each time?

_____   _____   _____   _____   _____

_____   _____   _____   _____   _____

Share and Show   MATH BOARD

THINK
What is the best way to count these objects?

Skip count. Count the roses by tens. Write how many.

✓ I.

_____   _____   _____   _____   _____

_____   _____   _____   _____

Name _____

Problem Solving

Skip count. Write how many.

2.

_____ grapes

3.

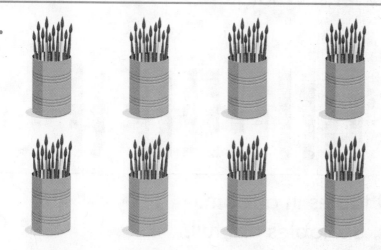

_____ paintbrushes

Use skip counting by tens to solve.
Write or draw to explain.

4. **H.O.T.** Vanessa swims
10 laps a day. How many
laps does she swim in 5 days?

_____ laps

5. **H.O.T.** **Multi-Step** There are
10 pencils in a packet. Justin
has 6 packets. He buys 3 more
packets. How many pencils
does he have?

_____ pencils

Daily Assessment Task

Mathematical Processes
Model • Reason • Communicate

Choose the correct answer.

6. **Analyze** Cody wants to make 11 trays of 10 tortillas. Skip count by tens. How many tortillas will he make?

○ 21   ○ 110   ○ 100

7. Jaimie uses base ten blocks to show a number. Skip count by tens. What is the number shown?

○ 10
○ 100
○ 120

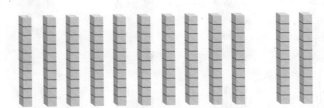

8. **Multi-Step** There are 10 tables in a room. Each table has 10 seats. Six tables are full. No one is sitting at the other tables. How many seats are empty?

○ 80   ○ 40   ○ 60

9. ⭐ **TEXAS Test Prep** Which number comes after 110 when skip counting by tens?

○ 120   ○ 80   ○ 100

 TAKE HOME ACTIVITY • Have your child explain how he or she would count how many objects are in 12 packets containing 10 objects each.

Name _____

10.5 Skip Count by Tens

Skip count. Count the fingers on the gloves by tens.
Write how many.

1.

_____ _____ _____ _____

_____ _____ _____ _____

_____ _____ _____ _____

Problem Solving Real World

Use skip counting by tens to solve.
Write or draw to explain.

2. Jason runs 10 laps around the track
   each day. How many laps does he
   run in 5 days?

_____ laps

Choose the correct answer.

3. Char's mom is making cupcakes.
   She can make 10 cupcakes with one pan.
   She makes 12 pans of cupcakes.
   How many cupcakes did Char's
   mom make?

   ○ 120   ○ 100   ○ 18

4. Paul counts his pennies. He draws a line
   for each group of 10 pennies he counts.
   How many pennies did Paul count?

   ○ 80   ○ 100   ○ 90

5. **Multi-Step** There are 10 party favors
   in each bag. Lonni buys 7 bags.
   Then he buys 3 more bags.
   How many favors did Lonni buy?

   ○ 70   ○ 100   ○ 30

6. Write the number that comes after 100
   when skip counting by tens.

   _____

Name _____

10.6 Count by Tens to 120

? Essential Question

How do numbers change as you count by tens to 120?

Explore

Start on 10. Count forward by tens.
Color each number as you say it.

1	2	3	4	5	6	7	8	9	10
11	12	13	14	15	16	17	18	19	20
21	22	23	24	25	26	27	28	29	30
31	32	33	34	35	36	37	38	39	40
41	42	43	44	45	46	47	48	49	50
51	52	53	54	55	56	57	58	59	60
61	62	63	64	65	66	67	68	69	70
71	72	73	74	75	76	77	78	79	80
81	82	83	84	85	86	87	88	89	90
91	92	93	94	95	96	97	98	99	100

Math Talk
Mathematical Processes

Which numbers in the hundred chart did you color? **Explain.**

FOR THE TEACHER • Read the following problem. When counting by tens, what number comes after 40?

Model and Draw

Start on 3. Count by tens. Write the numbers.

1	2	3	4	5	6	7	8	9	10
11	12	13	14	15	16	17	18	19	20
21	22	23	24	25	26	27	28	29	30
31	32	33	34	35	36	37	38	39	40
41	42	43	44	45	46	47	48	49	50
51	52	53	54	55	56	57	58	59	60
61	62	63	64	65	66	67	68	69	70
71	72	73	74	75	76	77	78	79	80
81	82	83	84	85	86	87	88	89	90
91	92	93	94	95	96	97	98	99	100
101	102	103	104	105	106	107	108	109	110
111	112	113	114	115	116	117	118	119	120

THINK
When you count by tens, each number is ten more.

3, 13, 23, 33, ____, ____, ____, ____, ____, ____, ____, ____

Share and Show

Use a Counting Chart to count by tens.
Write the numbers.

1. Start on 17.

   17, ____, ____, ____, ____, ____, ____, ____, ____

✓2. Start on 1.

   1, ____, ____, ____, ____, ____, ____, ____, ____

✓3. Start on 39.

   39, ____, ____, ____, ____, ____, ____, ____, ____

Name _____

Use a Counting Chart. Count by tens.
Write the numbers.

4. 40, _____, _____, _____, _____, _____, _____, _____

5. 15, _____, _____, _____, _____, _____, _____, _____

6. 28, _____, _____, _____, _____, _____, _____, _____

7. 6, _____, _____, _____, _____, _____, _____, _____

8. 14, _____, _____, _____, _____, _____, _____, _____

9. 32, _____, _____, _____, _____, _____, _____, _____

Solve.

10. **H.O.T.** If you start on 43 and count by tens, what number is after 73 and before 93?

_____

11. **H.O.T.** **Multi-Step** You say me when you start on 21 and count by tens. I am after 91. I am before 111. What number am I?

_____

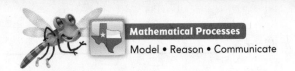

Choose the correct answer.

12. **Analyze** The giraffe eats 84 leaves. Then she eats 10 leaves off one tree and 10 off another. Count forward by tens. How many leaves does she eat?

   ○ 104   ○ 70   ○ 94

13. Gavin can count 10 numbers at a time. He starts at 6 and counts 11 times. Count forward by tens. What number does Gavin land on?

1	2	3	4	5	6	7	8	9	10
11	12	13	14	15	16	17	18	19	20
21	22	23	24	25	26	27	28	29	30
31	32	33	34	35	36	37	38	39	40
41	42	43	44	45	46	47	48	49	50
51	52	53	54	55	56	57	58	59	60
61	62	63	64	65	66	67	68	69	70
71	72	73	74	75	76	77	78	79	80
81	82	83	84	85	86	87	88	89	90
91	92	93	94	95	96	97	98	99	100
101	102	103	104	105	106	107	108	109	110
111	112	113	114	115	116	117	118	119	120

   ○ 96   ○ 116   ○ 17

14. **Multi-Step** Kay's fish tank only holds 120 fish. She adds 10 fish once a week. She does this for 2 weeks. How many more weeks will it take to fill the tank?

   ○ 12   ○ 10   ○ 8

15. ⭐ **TEXAS Test Prep** Count by tens. What numbers complete the count by tens sequence?

   3, 13, 23 _____, _____, 53

   ○ 24, 25 | ○ 33, 43 | ○ 63, 73

TAKE HOME ACTIVITY • Write these numbers: 2, 12, 22, 32, 42. Ask your child to tell you the next 5 numbers.

Homework and Practice

Name _____

10.6 Count by Tens to 120

Count by tens.
Write the numbers.

1. Start on 2.

   2, ____, ____, ____, ____, ____, ____, ____, ____

2. Start on 35.

   35, ____, ____, ____, ____, ____, ____, ____, ____

3. Start on 27.

   27, ____, ____, ____, ____, ____, ____, ____, ____

4. Start on 13.

   13, ____, ____, ____, ____, ____, ____, ____, ____

Problem Solving

Solve.

5. Libby has 49 pennies. She saves
   10 pennies a week for the next 6 weeks.
   Count forward by tens. How many
   pennies does Libby have now?

   _____ pennies

Choose the correct answer.

6. Rodney feeds the rabbits at the petting zoo. He gives them 19 carrots. Then he gives them 10 more carrots. How many carrots did Rodney give the rabbits?

  ○ 29   ○ 19   ○ 21

7. Shannon has 54 shells. She collects some more. She counts 5 more sets of 10 shells. How many shells does Shannon have now?

  ○ 64   ○ 74   ○ 104

8. **Multi-Step** Alan needs 100 dimes to fill his coin collection book. Each page holds 10 dimes. He fills 2 pages. How many more pages does he need to fill the book?

  ○ 10   ○ 8   ○ 2

9. Count by tens. What numbers are not shown?

6, 16, 26, ____, ____, ____, 66

  ○ 36, 46, 56
  ○ 27, 28, 29
  ○ 30, 40, 50

TEKS Algebraic
Reasoning—1.5.C
MATHEMATICAL PROCESSES
1.1.C, 1.1.F, 1.1.G

10.7 10 More, 10 Less

? **Essential Question**

How can you identify numbers that are 10 more or 10 less than a number?

Explore Real World

Use ▭▭▭▭▭ to solve. Draw quick pictures to show your work.

10 MARKERS

Pat

_____

Tony

_____

Jan

_____

FOR THE TEACHER • Read the following problem. Tony has 2 boxes of markers and 2 more markers. Pat has 10 fewer markers than Tony. Jan has 10 more markers than Tony. How many markers does each child have?

Math Talk
Mathematical Processes
What number has one less 10 than 12? Explain.

Model and Draw

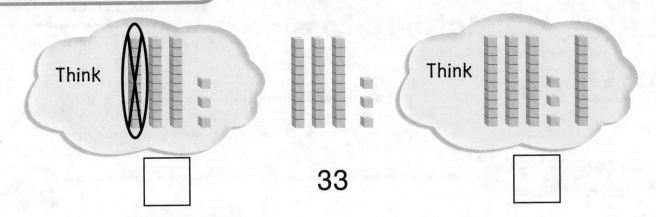

Think

23

____ is 10 less than 33.

33

Think

43

____ is 10 more than 33.

Share and Show

Use mental math. Write the numbers that are 10 less and 10 more.

1.
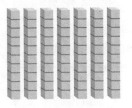

[ ] 70 [ ]

2.
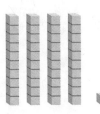

[ ] 41 [ ]

3. [ ] 58 [ ]

4. [ ] 66 [ ]

5. [ ] 24 [ ]

6. [ ] 86 [ ]

7. [ ] 37 [ ]

8. [ ] 15 [ ]

Problem Solving

Use mental math. Complete the chart.

	10 Less		10 More
9.	_____	39	_____
10.	_____	75	_____
11.	_____	90	_____
12.	_____	83	_____
13.	11	_____	_____

14. **H.O.T.** Solve. I have 89 rocks.
I want to collect 10 more.
How many rocks will I have then?

_____ rocks

15. **H.O.T.** **Multi-Step** Margo has
28 stamps. Chet has 10 more stamps
than Margo. Luis has 10 more stamps
than Chet. How many
stamps does Luis have?

_____ stamps

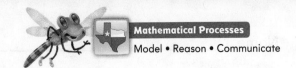

Mathematical Processes
Model • Reason • Communicate

Choose the correct answer.

16. You can practice flying at superhero training camp. You fly up 86 feet. Then you fly up 10 more feet. How far are you above the ground?

○ 106 feet   ○ 96 feet   ○ 76 feet

17. Display Look at the chart. What are the unknown numbers?

10 Less	Number	10 More
	97	

○ 87 and 107   ○ 96 and 98   ○ 107 and 117

18. Multi-Step Stacey has 102 pennies. Jamal gives her 10 more pennies. She loses 2 pennies. Then Stacey gives 10 pennies back to Jamal. How many pennies does Stacey have?

○ 112   ○ 100   ○ 92

19. ⭐ **TEXAS Test Prep** What number is 10 less than 76?

○ 66   ○ 86   ○ 75

TAKE HOME ACTIVITY • Write a two-digit number, such as 25, 40, or 81. Ask your child to identify the numbers that are ten less than and ten more than that number. Repeat with other numbers.

10.7 10 More, 10 Less

Use mental math. Write the numbers that are 10 less and 10 more.

1.

   [ ] 40 [ ]

2.

   [ ] 31 [ ]

3. [ ] 77 [ ]

4. [ ] 13 [ ]

Problem Solving Real World

Solve. Draw or explain your answer.

5. A bird lands on a branch of a tree. The branch is 33 feet above the ground. Then the bird flies to a branch that is 10 feet higher. How far is the bird above the ground?

   _____ feet

Choose the correct answer.

6. A group of hikers camp 82 feet up on a mountain. The next night they camp 10 feet higher. How far up the mountain did they camp?

○ 92 feet   ○ 72 feet   ○ 102 feet

7. **Multi-Step** Carl has 87 toy cars. He gives 10 cars to Elena. Then Mark gives Carl 10 cars. How many cars does Carl have now?

○ 77   ○ 67   ○ 87

8. What number is 10 less than 34?

     ○ 24

     ○ 4

     ○ 44

9. Look at the chart. Write the unknown numbers.

10 Less	Number	10 More
	104	

Name _____

Module 10 Assessment

Use the counting chart.
Count forward by ones.
Write the numbers. ⬇ TEKS 1.5.A

1	2	3	4	5	6	7	8	9	10
11	12	13	14	15	16	17	18	19	20
21	22	23	24	25	26	27	28	29	30
31	32	33	34	35	36	37	38	39	40
41	42	43	44	45	46	47	48	49	50
51	52	53	54	55	56	57	58	59	60
61	62	63	64	65	66	67	68	69	70
71	72	73	74	75	76	77	78	79	80
81	82	83	84	85	86	87	88	89	90
91	92	93	94	95	96	97	98	99	100
101	102	103	104	105	106	107	108	109	110
111	112	113	114	115	116	117	118	119	120

1. 52, 53, _____, _____, _____, _____

2. 115, 116, _____, _____, _____, _____

Use the counting chart.
Count backward by ones.
Write the numbers. ⬇ TEKS 1.5.A

3. 74, 73, _____, _____, _____, _____

4. 112, 111, _____, _____, _____, _____

Use the counting chart.
Count by tens.
Write the numbers. ⬇ TEKS 1.5.C

5. 60, 70, _____, _____, _____, _____

6. 55, 65, _____, _____, _____, _____

Choose the correct answer.

7. Which number begins the skip count
by twos sequence? TEKS 1.5.B

- ○ 4
- ○ 2
- ○ 1

8. Which number begins the skip count
by fives sequence? TEKS 1.5.B

- ○ 5
- ○ 1
- ○ 10

9. Which number begins the skip count
by tens sequence? TEKS 1.5.B

- ○ 20
- ○ 1
- ○ 10

10. Which number is ten more than 100? TEKS 1.5.C

- ○ 110
- ○ 101
- ○ 90

11.1 PROBLEM SOLVING • Model Addition

? Essential Question

How do you solve addition problems by making a model?

🔑 Unlock the Problem 🌎 Real World

Hanna has 4 red flowers in a .
She puts 2 more flowers in the .
How many flowers are in the ?
How can you use a model to find out?

Read	Plan
What information am I given?	**What is my plan or strategy?**
_____ red flowers	I can _____
_____ more flowers	_____.

Solve

Show how you solve the problem.

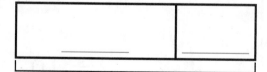

$4 + 2 = \underline{}$

HOME CONNECTION • Your child can model the concepts of joining, adding to, and putting together. He or she used a model to show the problems and solve.

© Houghton Mifflin Harcourt Publishing Company

Try Another Problem

Use to help you. Complete the model and the number sentence.

• What information am I given?
• What is my plan or strategy?

1. There are 7 dogs in the park. Then 1 more dog joins them. How many dogs are in the park now?

| 7 | 1 |

7 + 1 = ___

2. Some birds are sitting in the tree. Four more birds sit in the tree. Then there are 9 birds. How many birds were in the tree before?

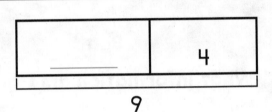

9

___ + 4 = 9

3. There are 4 horses in the field. Some more horses run to the field. Now there are 10 horses in the field. How many horses ran to the field?

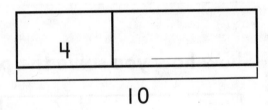

10

4 + ___ = 10

Math Talk
Mathematical Processes

How does a model help you solve Exercise 1? Explain.

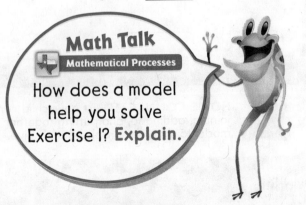

408 four hundred eight

© Houghton Mifflin Harcourt Publishing Company

Share and Show

Use 🔲➕🔲 to help you. Complete
the model and the number sentence.

✓4. Luis has 12 crayons.
5 of the crayons are red.
The rest are blue. How
many crayons are blue?

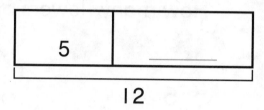

$$5 + \_\_\_ = 12$$

Problem Solving

5. **H.O.T.** Some ducks
are swimming in a
pond. 3 more ducks
swim in the pond.
Then there are 6 ducks
in the pond. How many ducks
were in the pond before?

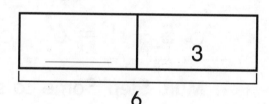

$$\_\_\_ + 3 = 6$$

6. **H.O.T.** Multi-Step

_____ bugs are flying.
_____ more bugs fly
with them. Now there
are 10 bugs flying.

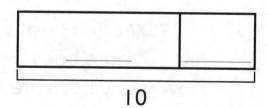

$$\_\_\_ \bigcirc \_\_\_ \bigcirc 10$$

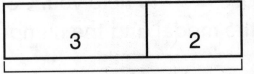

Mathematical Processes
Model • Reason • Communicate

Use . Choose the correct answer.

7. Use Diagrams Cho sees 3 red flowers. Ki sees 2 yellow flowers. How many flowers are there?

3	2

○ 5   ○ 3   ○ 2

8. Ben has 5 books. Kelli has 3 books. Which number sentence shows how many books there are?

5	3

○ 5 + 1 = 6   ○ 5 + 3 = 8   ○ 5 + 2 = 7

9. Multi-Step Some cats sit on a fence. 4 cats join them. Now there are 8 cats on the fence. How many cats were on the fence before?

___	4

8

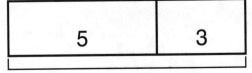

○ 3   ○ 2   ○ 4

10. ⭐ **TEXAS Test Prep** 6 bees are in the hive. 3 more bees fly into the hive. How many bees are in the hive now?

6	3

○ 3   ○ 9   ○ 4

TAKE HOME ACTIVITY • Have your child describe each of the parts of a model using the number sentence 7 + 3 = 10.

© Houghton Mifflin Harcourt Publishing Company • Image Credits: (t), (c) ©Photodisc/Getty Images; (b) ©Artville/Getty Images

Name _____

11.1 PROBLEM SOLVING • Model Addition

Complete the model and number sentence.

1. There are 4 plates on the table. You put 3 more plates on the table. How many plates are on the table now?

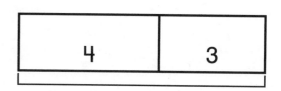

$4 + 3 = \underline{\quad}$

2. 8 fish swim in a pond. Some more fish swim into the pond. Now there are 11 fish in the pond. How many fish swam into the pond?

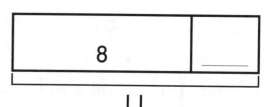

$8 + \underline{\quad} = 11$

Problem Solving Real World

3. Some bees are flying around a flower. 7 more bees fly with them. Now there are 13 bees flying. How many bees were flying before?

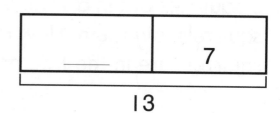

$\underline{\quad} + 7 = 13$

Choose the correct answer.

4. Jerry sees 5 blue cars. Tina sees 6 red cars. How many cars are there?

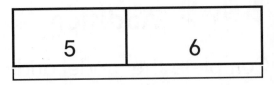

○ 5   ○ 11   ○ 6

5. Cal has 7 pens. Zeb has 2 pens. Which number sentence shows how many pens there are?

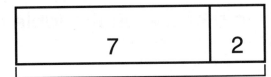

○ 7 + 2 = 9   ○ 7 − 2 = 5   ○ 7 + 1 = 8

6. Casey has some shells. Sal gives Casey 4 shells. Now Casey has 6 shells. How many shells did Casey have before?

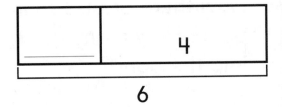

○ 4   ○ 6   ○ 2

7. 3 squirrels are in a tree. 5 more squirrels join them. How many squirrels are in the tree now?

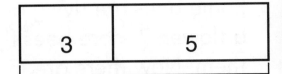

○ 8

○ 7

○ 9

TEKS Algebraic
Reasoning—1.5.D
Also 1.3.B
MATHEMATICAL PROCESSES
1.1.B, 1.1.D

11.2 PROBLEM SOLVING • Model Subtraction

 Essential Question

How do you solve subtraction problems by making a model?

Unlock the Problem

Tom has 6 crayons in a box.
He takes 2 crayons out of the box.
How many crayons are in the box now?
How can you use a model to find out?

Read	Plan
What information am I given?	**What is my plan or strategy?**
____ crayons in a box	I can _____
____ crayons taken out	_____.

Solve

Show how you solve the problem.

$6 - 2 =$ ____

HOME CONNECTION • Your child used a model to help him or her understand and solve the subtraction problem.

Try Another Problem

Use 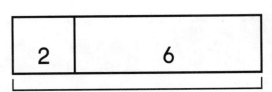 to help you. Complete the model and the number sentence.

• What information am I given?
• What is my plan or strategy?

1. There are 10 stickers.
   7 stickers are orange.
   The rest are brown.
   How many stickers
   are brown?

7	

10

$10 - 7 = \underline{\quad}$

2. Some birds were in
   the tree. 2 birds flew
   away. Then there
   were 6 birds. How
   many birds were in
   the tree before?

2	6

_____

$\underline{\quad} - 2 = 6$

3. There were 5 cars.
   Some cars drove away.
   Then there was I car.
   How many cars
   drove away?

	1

5

$5 - \underline{\quad} = 1$

Math Talk
Mathematical Processes

What does each part of the model show? Explain.

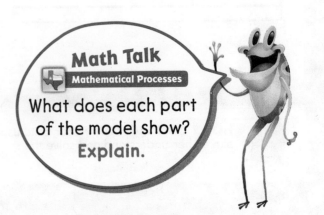

Name _____

Use  to help you. Complete the model and the number sentence.

☑ 4. Some goats were in the field. 3 goats ran away. Then there were 4 goats. How many goats were in the field before?

3	4

_____ − 3 = 4

Problem Solving

5. **H.O.T.** Write your own story problem using the model.

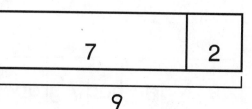

_____

_ _ _ _ _ _ _ _ _ _ _ _ _

_____

_ _ _ _ _ _ _ _ _ _ _ _ _

6. **H.O.T.** Multi-Step
Complete the model. Write your own story problem using the model.

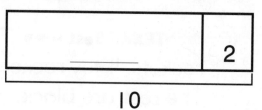

_____

_ _ _ _ _ _ _ _ _ _ _ _ _

_____

_ _ _ _ _ _ _ _ _ _ _ _ _

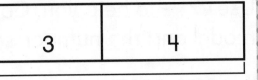

Daily Assessment Task

Use ▣ ▫. Choose the correct answer.

7. Use Diagrams Peg buys some bananas. Dan eats 3 bananas. Now there are 4 bananas left. How many bananas did Peg buy?

3	4

○ 4   ○ 7   ○ 6

8. Mari has 11 balloons. 6 balloons are blue. The rest are orange. How many balloons are orange?

6	_____

11

○ 5   ○ 6   ○ 11

9. Marta had 7 grapes. She ate some. Now she has 3. Which number sentence shows how many grapes Marta ate?

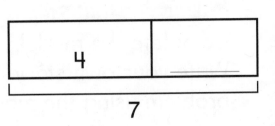

○ $7 - 5 = 2$ | ○ $7 - 6 = 1$ | ○ $7 - 4 = 3$

10. ⭐ **TEXAS Test Prep** There are 7 toy rockets. 4 toy rockets are red. The rest are black. How many toy rockets are black?

4	_____

7

○ 3   ○ 7   ○ 4

TAKE HOME ACTIVITY • Ask your child to describe what the bottom part of a model means when subtracting.

TEKS Algebraic Reasoning—1.5.D
Also 1.3.B
MATHEMATICAL PROCESSES 1.1.B, 1.1.D

Name _____

11.2 PROBLEM SOLVING • Model Subtraction

Complete the model and number sentence.

1. There are 9 cups. 3 cups are white. The rest are red. How many cups are red?

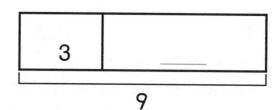

$$9 - 3 = \underline{}$$

2. 8 mice were playing. Some mice ran away. Then there were 2 mice. How many mice ran away?

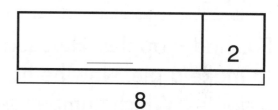

$$8 - 2 = \underline{}$$

Problem Solving

3. **Multi Step** Complete the model. Write your own story problem using the model.

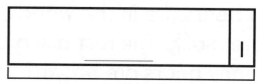

_____

_____

_____

_____

Choose the correct answer.

4. Tad has 6 shirts. 2 shirts are white. The other shirts are blue. How many shirts are blue?

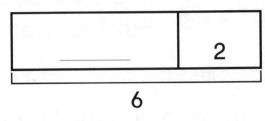

	2
6	

○ 8   ○ 6   ○ 4

5. Tom had some pencils. He gave 7 pencils to friends. Now he has 3 pencils. How many pencils did Tom have?

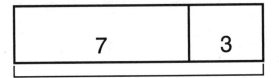

7	3

○ 10   ○ 4   ○ 5

6. Pat had 9 apples. He used some to make a pie. Now he has 5 apples. Which number sentence shows how many apples Pat used?

○ 9 − 7 = 2   ○ 9 − 4 = 5   ○ 9 − 6 = 3

7. 11 bears are in the woods. 6 bears are black. The rest are brown. How many bears are brown?

○ 7
○ 6
○ 5

6	
11	

Name _____

11.3
HANDS ON
Subtract to Compare

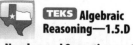
TEKS Algebraic Reasoning—1.5.D
Number and Operations—1.3.B
MATHEMATICAL PROCESSES 1.1.D

? Essential Question

How can you use models to compare and subtract?

Explore Real World

Use ● to show the problem. Draw the ●.
Model the problem using the model.

Math Talk
Mathematical Processes

Explain how you find how many more puzzle pieces Mindy has than David.

FOR THE TEACHER • Read the problem. Mindy has 8 puzzle pieces. David has 5 puzzle pieces. How many more puzzle pieces does Mindy have than David?

Model and Draw

James has 4 stones. Heather has 7 stones. How many fewer stones does James have than Heather?

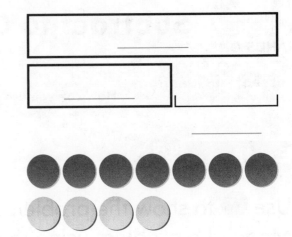

____ ◯ ____ ◯ ____

____ fewer stones

Share and Show

Use ⬤ to show the problem. Use the model to solve. Write the number sentence. Then write how many.

✓1. Abby has 8 stamps. Ben has 6 stamps. How many more stamps does Abby have than Ben?

____ more stamps

____ ◯ ____ ◯ ____

✓2. Tanner has 3 books. Vicky has 6 books. How many fewer books does Tanner have than Vicky?

____ fewer books

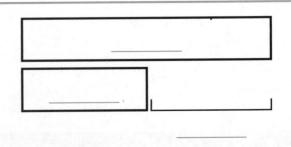

____ ◯ ____ ◯ ____

420 four hundred twenty

Name _____

Problem Solving

Use ⬤ to show the problem. Use the model to solve. Write the number sentence. Then write how many.

3. Sally has 5 feathers. James has 2 feathers. How many more feathers does Sally have than James?

_____ more feathers

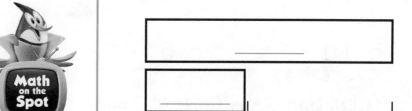

___ ◯ ___ ◯ ___

4. **H.O.T.** Pam has 4 marbles. Rick has 10 marbles. How many fewer marbles does Pam have than Rick?

_____ fewer marbles

Math on the Spot

___ ◯ ___ ◯ ___

5. **H.O.T.** **Multi-Step** Kyle has 6 keys. Kyle has 4 more keys than Lee. How many keys does Lee have?

_____ keys

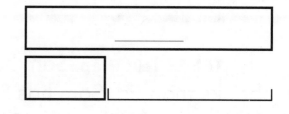

___ ◯ ___ ◯ ___

Daily Assessment Task

Mathematical Processes
Model • Reason • Communicate

Use ⬤. Choose the correct answer.

6. Use Diagrams Tony eats 3 treats. Milo eats 5 treats. How many more treats does Milo eat than Tony?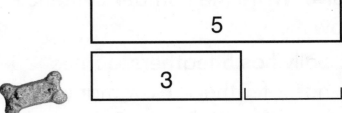

○ 2   ○ 8   ○ 3

7. Mandy has 10 beads. Amy has 4 beads. How many fewer beads does Amy have than Mandy?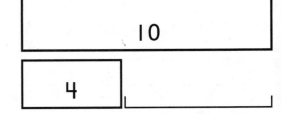

○ 10   ○ 5   ○ 6

8. Multi-Step Sara finds 9 shells. She finds 4 more shells than Josh. Which number sentence shows how many shells Josh found?

○ 9 − 3 = 6   ○ 11 − 2 = 9   ○ 9 − 4 = 5

9. ⭐ **TEXAS Test Prep** Sam has three more books than Ed. Sam has 8 books. How many books does Ed have?

○ 5
○ 11
○ 8

 TAKE HOME ACTIVITY • Ask your child to solve this problem. Liz picks 15 flowers. 7 are pink. The rest are yellow. How many are yellow?

Name _____

11.3
HANDS ON

Subtract to Compare

Use the model to solve. Write the number sentence. Then write how many.

1. 9 bees are flying. 4 bees are on flowers. How many more bees are flying than on flowers?

____ more bees

___ ◯ ___ ◯ ___

2. Vince has 7 toys. Pat has 4 toys. How many fewer toys does Pat have than Vince?

____ fewer toys

___ ◯ ___ ◯ ___

Problem Solving *Real World*

3. Tim has 8 rulers. Chad has 4 rulers. How many fewer rulers does Chad have than Tim?

____ fewer rulers

___ ◯ ___ ◯ ___

Lesson Check

Choose the correct answer.

4. Fido has 12 bones. Champ has 9 bones. How many more bones does Fido have than Champ?

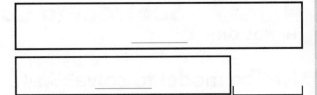

   ○ 9   ○ 3   ○ 12

5. A big squirrel ate 8 nuts. A small squirrel ate 2 nuts. How many fewer nuts did the small squirrel eat?

   ○ 6   ○ 10   ○ 4

6. **Multi-Step** Farmer Grey has 10 chicks. He has 3 more chicks than Farmer Brown. Which number sentence shows how many chicks Farmer Brown has?

   ○ $10 - 6 = 4$ ○ $7 - 3 = 4$ ○ $10 - 3 = 7$

7. Lou has 7 marbles. Kim has 2 marbles. How many fewer marbles does Kim have than Lou?

   ○ 9   ○ 5   ○ 7

11.4 PROBLEM SOLVING • Add or Subtract

TEKS Algebraic Reasoning—1.5.D
Also 1.3.B
MATHEMATICAL PROCESSES
1.1.B, 1.1.D

 Essential Question

How can making a model help you solve a problem?

🔑 Unlock the Problem

Nicole sees 16 turtles on the beach. Some turtles swim away. There are 9 turtles still on the beach. How many turtles swim away?

Read	Plan
What information am I given?	**What is my plan or strategy?**
_____ turtles	I can _____
__?__ swim away	_____.
_____ turtles still on the beach	

Solve

Show how you solve the problem.

```
┌──────────────┬──────────┐
│              │    9     │
└──────────────┴──────────┘
        16
```

16 turtles _____ swim away  9 turtles still on the beach

 HOME CONNECTION • Your child made a model to visualize the problem. The model helps your child see what part of the problem to find.

Model and Draw

Make a model to solve.

Use 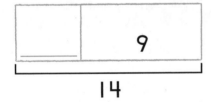 to help you.

1. There are 4 rabbits in the field. Some more rabbits come. Now there are 12 rabbits. How many rabbits come to the field?

4	

12

4 rabbits   _____ rabbits come   12 rabbits in the field

---

2. There are 14 birds in a tree. Some birds fly away. There are 9 birds still in the tree. How many birds fly away?

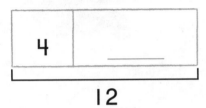

	9

14

14 birds   _____ birds fly away   9 birds still in the tree

Math Talk

Mathematical Processes

Explain how to find the unknown number.

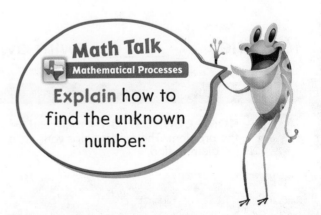

Name _____

Make a model to solve.
Use ▪ ▫ to help you.

☑ **3.** There are 20 ducks in the pond.
Then 10 ducks swim away.
How many ducks are still
in the pond?

10	_____

20

20 ducks   10 swim away   ____ ducks still in the pond

Problem Solving

4. **H.O.T.**   3 eagles land in the
trees. Now 12 eagles are in
the trees. How many eagles
were in the trees to start?

_____	3

12

____ eagles   3 eagles land   12 eagles in the trees

5. **H.O.T.**   **Multi-Step** 8 squirrels
are in the park. The same number
of squirrels join them. How many
squirrels are in the park now?

8	_____

_____

8 squirrels ____ squirrels join them ____ squirrels in the park

Use objects to solve the problem. Choose the correct answer.

6. There are 6 children at the big tree. More children come to the tree. Now there are 14 children. How many children come to the tree?

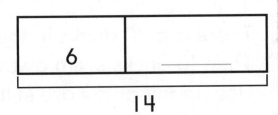

| 6 | _____ |

14

○ 9　　　　○ 6　　　　○ 8

7. **Use Diagrams** There are 15 birds in the tree. 7 birds are blue. The other birds are brown. How many birds are brown?

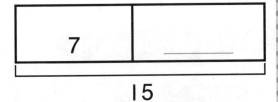

| 7 | _____ |

15

○ 8　　　　○ 6　　　　○ 7

8. There are 4 more blue birds than red birds. There are 12 blue birds. How many red birds are there?

○ 9　　　　○ 16　　　　○ 8

9. ⭐ **TEXAS Test Prep** There are 13 fish in the tank. Some fish swim behind the rock. There are 8 fish in front of the rock. How many fish are behind the rock?

○ 4　　　　○ 6　　　　○ 5

TAKE HOME ACTIVITY • Ask your child to tell you how he or she solved a problem on this page.

428 four hundred twenty-eight

11.4 PROBLEM SOLVING • Add or Subtract

Make a model to solve.

1. There are 13 frogs by the pond. 6 frogs hop away. How many frogs are still by the pond?

6	____

13

13 frogs   6 hop away   ____ frogs still by the pond

---

2. Ginny blows up 9 balloons. Now there are 18 balloons. How many balloons were there before?

____	9

18

____ balloons before   9 balloons   18 balloons now

Problem Solving Real World

3. Multi-Step 6 friends play ball in the park. The same number of friends join them. How many friends are in the park now?

6	____

____

6 friends   ____ friends join them   ____ friends now

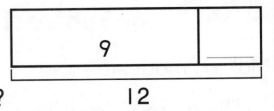
Choose the correct answer.

4. There are 9 desks in the room. The teacher brings in more desks. Now there are 12 desks. How many desks did the teacher bring in?

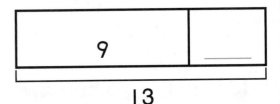

○ 4 ○ 6 ○ 3

5. A house has 9 more small windows than big windows. The house has 13 windows. How many big windows does it have?

○ 4 ○ 5 ○ 6

6. 7 worms are in the garden. 6 more worms crawl over. How many worms are in the garden now?

○ 14 ○ 12 ○ 13

7. There are 16 birds in a tree. Some birds fly away. There are 9 birds left in the tree. How many birds flew away?

○ 9 ○ 7 ○ 8

Module II Assessment

Concepts and Skills

Use 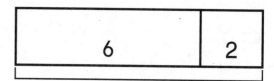. Complete the model and the number sentence.

1. 6 bunnies sit in the grass. 2 more bunnies join them. How many bunnies are in the grass now? ▶ TEKS 1.5.D

| 6 | 2 |

$6 + 2 = $ _____

2. There are 2 people in the house. Some more people go in the house. Now there are 6 people in the house. How many people go in the house? ▶ TEKS 1.5.D

| 2 | _____ |

6

$2 + $ _____ $ = 6$

3. Jennifer has 3 pennies. Brad has 9 pennies. How many fewer pennies does Jennifer have than Brad? ▶ TEKS 1.5.D

_____ ◯ _____ ◯ _____

4. There are 9 beads.
5 beads are pink.
The rest are yellow.
How many beads
are yellow? TEKS 1.5.D

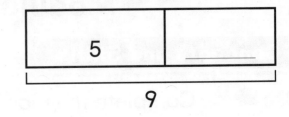

- ○ 5
- ○ 9
- ○ 4

5. Mandy has 2 rocks.
Peter has 8 rocks.
How many more
rocks does Peter
have than Mandy? TEKS 1.5.D

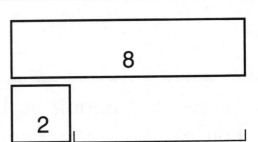

- ○ $8 - 2 = 6$
- ○ $6 - 2 = 4$
- ○ $8 - 3 = 5$

6. Pat picks 18 flowers.
9 are yellow.
The rest are pink.
How many are pink? TEKS 1.5.D

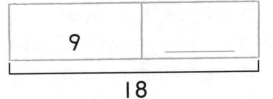

- ○ 8
- ○ 9
- ○ 7

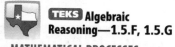
Name _____

ALGEBRA

Add in Any Order

 Essential Question

What happens if you change the order of the addends when you add?

Explore

Hands On

Use 🖍 and 🖍. Color to model
the problem. Write the addition sentence.

⬜⬜⬜⬜⬜⬜⬜⬜⬜⬜⬜⬜⬜⬜⬜

____ + ____ = ____

Use 🖍 and 🖍. Color to change the order.
Write the addition sentence.

⬜⬜⬜⬜⬜⬜⬜⬜⬜⬜⬜⬜⬜⬜⬜

____ + ____ = ____

Math Talk
Mathematical Processes

Explain how knowing
the fact 7 + 8 helps
you find 8 + 7.

 FOR THE TEACHER • Read the problem. George
sees 7 blue birds and 8 red birds. How many birds
does he see? Help children work through
changing the order of the addends.

Module 12

four hundred thirty-three **433**

If you use the same addends, what other fact can you write?

$$5 + 6 +$$

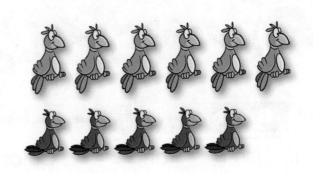

Share and Show

Add. Change the order of the addends. Add again.

1.
$$8 + 9 +$$

2.
$$6 + 7 +$$

3.
$$7 + 5 +$$

4.
$$2 + 8 +$$

✓5.
$$9 + 2 +$$

✓6.
$$8 + 4 +$$

Name _____

Problem Solving

Add. Change the order of
the addends. Add again.

7.
$$\begin{array}{r} 9 \\ + 6 \end{array}$$ $\Box$ $+$ $\Box$
$\Box$

8.
$$\begin{array}{r} 7 \\ + 9 \end{array}$$ $\Box$ $+$ $\Box$
$\Box$

9.
$$\begin{array}{r} 8 \\ + 3 \end{array}$$ $\Box$ $+$ $\Box$
$\Box$

10.
$$\begin{array}{r} 5 \\ + 9 \end{array}$$ $\Box$ $+$ $\Box$
$\Box$

11.
$$\begin{array}{r} 4 \\ + 5 \end{array}$$ $\Box$ $+$ $\Box$
$\Box$

12.
$$\begin{array}{r} 8 \\ + 5 \end{array}$$ $\Box$ $+$ $\Box$
$\Box$

13. **H.O.T.** Anna has two groups of pennies.
She has 10 pennies in all. When she
changes the order of the addends,
the addition sentence is the same.
What sentence can Anna write?   ____ = ____ + ____

14. **H.O.T. Multi-Step** If Adam knows $4 + 7 = 11$,
what other addition fact does he know?
Write the new fact in the box. Tell how
Adam knows the new fact.

_____

_ _

_____

Mathematical Processes
Model • Reason • Communicate

Choose the correct answer.

15. The number sentence $4 + 5 = 9$ tells about 9 snails racing up trees. Which number sentence shows the addends in a different order?

○ $3 + 6 = 9$
○ $2 + 3 = 5$
○ $5 + 4 = 9$

16. **Analyze** Joey uses the number sentence $3 + 7 = 10$ to tell about his toy trucks. What other number sentence tells about his trucks?

○ $6 + 4 = 10$
○ $7 + 3 = 10$
○ $4 + 3 = 7$

17. John wrote the number sentence $5 + 3 = 8$. Which shows the same addends in a different order?

○ $3 + 5 = 8$
○ $5 + 5 = 10$
○ $5 + 8 = 13$

18. ⭐ **TEXAS Test Prep** Which shows the same addends in a different order?

$$9 + 3 = 12$$

○ $6 + 3 = 9$
○ $3 + 9 = 12$
○ $4 + 8 = 12$

TAKE HOME ACTIVITY • Ask your child to explain what happens to the sum when you change the order of the addends.

12.1 ALGEBRA Add in Any Order

Add. Change the order of the addends.
Add again.

1.
$$\begin{array}{r} 5 \\ + 8 \end{array}$$ + □ = □

2.
$$\begin{array}{r} 7 \\ + 2 \end{array}$$ + □ = □

3.
$$\begin{array}{r} 6 \\ + 4 \end{array}$$ + □ = □

4.
$$\begin{array}{r} 9 \\ + 3 \end{array}$$ + □ = □

5.
$$\begin{array}{r} 7 \\ + 8 \end{array}$$ + □ = □

6.
$$\begin{array}{r} 8 \\ + 6 \end{array}$$ + □ = □

Problem Solving Real World

7. If Lorena knows that $6 + 9 = 15$, what other addition fact does she know? Write the new fact in the box. Tell how Lorena knows the new fact.

_____

- - - - - - - - - - - - - - - - - - - -

_____

Choose the correct answer.

8. Alice uses the number sentence $5 + 9 = 14$ to tell about the number of laps she ran. Which number sentence shows the addends in a different order?

○ $5 + 8 = 14$ ○ $9 + 5 = 14$ ○ $4 + 5 = 9$

9. The number sentence $3 + 6 = 9$ tells about 9 pieces of fruit. What other number sentence tells about the same pieces fruit?

○ $3 + 2 = 5$ ○ $4 + 4 = 8$ ○ $6 + 3 = 9$

10. **Multi-Step** Jake writes an addition sentence. When he changes the order of the addends, the addition sentence is the same. Which addition sentence can Jake write?

○ $3 + 5 = 8$ ○ $8 + 8 = 16$ ○ $5 + 6 = 11$

11. Which shows the same addends in a different order?

$$\boxed{4 + 9 = 13}$$

○ $9 + 4 = 13$ ○ $13 - 4 = 9$ ○ $7 + 6 = 13$

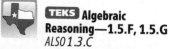

TEKS Algebraic Reasoning—1.5.F, 1.5.G
ALSO 1.3.C
MATHEMATICAL PROCESSES
1.1.E, 1.1.F, 1.1.G

12.2
HANDS ON ALGEBRA

Add 3 Numbers

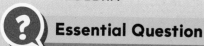

? Essential Question

How can you add three addends?

Explore Real World

Use to model the problem.
Draw to show your work.

_____ birds

FOR THE TEACHER • Read the following problem. Kelly sees 7 birds. Bill sees 2 birds. Joe sees 3 birds. How many birds do they see?

Math Talk
Mathematical Processes

Which two addends did you add first? Explain.

$2 + 3 + 1 =$ _____

> You can change which two addends you add first. The sum stays the same.

Add 2 and 3. Then add 1.

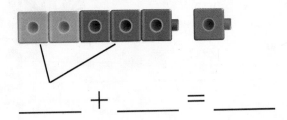

_____ + _____ = _____

Add 3 and 1. Then add 2.

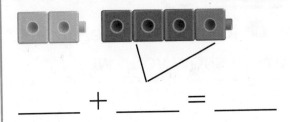

_____ + _____ = _____

Share and Show

Use ▪ ▪ ▪ to change which two addends you add first. Complete the addition sentences.

✓1. $5 + 2 + 3 =$ _____

_____ + _____ = _____   _____ + _____ = _____

✓2. $3 + 4 + 6 =$ _____

_____ + _____ = _____   _____ + _____ = _____

Problem Solving

Look at the . Complete the addition
sentences showing two ways to find the sum.

3. 7 + 3 + 1 = ____

____ + ____ = ____   ____ + ____ = ____

4. 3 + 6 + 3 = ____

____ + ____ = ____   ____ + ____ = ____

5. **H.O.T.** I used
■ ■ ■ to
model 3 addends.
Use my model.
Write the
3 addends.

My Model
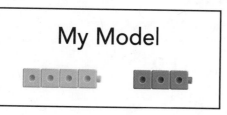

____ + ____ + ____ = 7

6. Without adding, circle the
group of numbers that you
think will have the greater sum.

5				4	
	8				3
9				5	

How did you estimate?

_____

_____

Mathematical Processes

Model • Reason • Communicate

Use . Choose the correct answer.

7. There are 7 camels in the desert.
There are 5 camels on the hill.
There are 3 camels by the water.
How many camels are there?

○ 17   ○ 15   ○ 10

8. Apply There are 6 people wearing jeans.
There are 2 people wearing dresses.
There are 4 people wearing shorts.
How many people are there?

○ 12   ○ 8   ○ 17

9. Multi-Step There are 6 books on the shelf.
Julie puts 4 books on the shelf.
Michelle puts 5 books on the shelf.
Then Julie puts 3 more books on the shelf.
How many books are on the shelf?

○ 10   ○ 19   ○ 18

10. ⭐ **TEXAS Test Prep** What is the sum for
$2 + 2 + 8$?

○ 20   ○ 11   ○ 12

TAKE HOME ACTIVITY • Have your child draw to
show two ways to add the numbers 2, 4, and 6.

12.2 Add 3 Numbers

HANDS ON ALGEBRA

Look at the ▢+▢+▢ to change which addends you add first. Complete the addition sentences.

1. $6 + 4 + 2 =$ _____

_____ + _____ = _____   _____ + _____ = _____

2. $6 + 1 + 2 =$ _____

_____ + _____ = _____   _____ + _____ = _____

Problem Solving Real World

3. **Multi-Step** Choose three numbers from 2 to 5. Write the numbers as addends in an addition sentence. Show two ways to find the sum.

_____ + _____ + _____ = _____

_____ + _____ = _____   _____ + _____ = _____

Choose the correct answer.

4. There are 5 dogs. There are 7 cats. There are 3 hamsters. How many pets are there?

○ 10   ○ 12   ○ 15

5. Children brought toys to school. 3 children brought balls. 6 children brought games. 8 children brought trucks. How many toys did the children bring to school?

○ 17   ○ 14   ○ 9

6. Without adding, circle the group of numbers that you think will have the greatest sum.

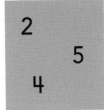
2
  5
4

7
  9
8

5
  5
5

Explain how you made your estimate.

_____

_____

_____

TEKS Algebraic
Reasoning—1.5.F, 1.5.G
Also 1.3.C
MATHEMATICAL PROCESSES
1.1.E, 1.1.F, 1.1.G

12.3
ALGEBRA

Add 3 Numbers

 Essential Question

How can you group numbers to add three addends?

Explore

Listen to the problem. Show two ways
to group and add the numbers.

| 3 | 6 | 3 |

 FOR THE TEACHER • Read the following
problem. There are 3 children at one table.
There are 6 children at another table.
There are 3 children in line. How many
children are there?

Math Talk
Mathematical Processes

Describe the two
ways you grouped the
numbers to add.

Model and Draw

You can group the addends in any order, and in different ways to find the sum.

Add 8 and 2 to use the strategy make a ten. Then add 10 and 6.

Add 6 and 2 to use the strategy count on. Then add doubles 8 and 8.

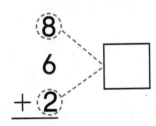

$$\begin{array}{r} 8 \\ 6 \\ + 2 \end{array} \rightarrow \square$$

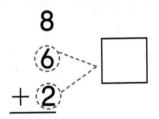

$$\begin{array}{r} 8 \\ 6 \\ + 2 \end{array} \rightarrow \square$$

Share and Show

MATH BOARD

Choose a strategy. Circle two addends to add first. Write the sum. Then find the total sum. Then use a different strategy and add again.

THINK
Use count on, doubles, doubles plus one, doubles minus one, or make a ten to add.

1.
$$\begin{array}{r} 6 \\ 4 \\ + 2 \end{array} \square \qquad \begin{array}{r} 6 \\ 4 \\ + 2 \end{array} \square$$

2.
$$\begin{array}{r} 3 \\ 4 \\ + 4 \end{array} \square \qquad \begin{array}{r} 3 \\ 4 \\ + 4 \end{array} \square$$

✓3.
$$\begin{array}{r} 2 \\ 5 \\ + 0 \end{array} \square \qquad \begin{array}{r} 2 \\ 5 \\ + 0 \end{array} \square$$

✓4.
$$\begin{array}{r} 5 \\ 4 \\ + 5 \end{array} \square \qquad \begin{array}{r} 5 \\ 4 \\ + 5 \end{array} \square$$

Name _____

Choose a strategy. Circle two addends
to add first. Write the sum.

5.	6.	7.	8.
8 2 + 2	6 0 + 8	3 4 + 6	2 3 + 7

9.	10.	11.	12.
7 7 + 2	9 9 + 1	5 4 + 4	5 5 + 5

H.O.T. Write the missing addends. Add.

13.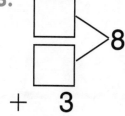

$+$ 3

14.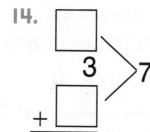

$+$

Draw a picture. Complete the number sentence.

15. **H.O.T.** Multi-Step Kathy sees 13 fish in the
tank. 6 fish are gold. The rest are blue or
red. How many of each could she see?

_____ + _____ + 6 = 13 fish

Mathematical Processes
Model • Reason • Communicate

Choose the correct answer.

16. Apply Jerry has 4 red caps. He has 6 green caps. He has 3 blue caps. How many caps does Jerry have?

○ 14   ○ 10   ○ 13

17. Ty sees 5 blue kites. He sees 7 red kites. He sees 4 purple kites. How many kites does he see?

○ 16   ○ 12   ○ 19

18. Multi-Step Ben has 7 white blocks. He has 7 blue blocks. He has some red blocks. Ben has 16 blocks in all. How many red blocks does Ben have?

○ 1   ○ 4   ○ 2

19. ⭐ **TEXAS Test Prep** What is the sum of 7 + 4 + 3?

○ 7

○ 13

○ 14

TAKE HOME ACTIVITY • Have your child explain how he or she can add the numbers 3, 2, and 5.

12.3 Add 3 Numbers

ALGEBRA

Choose a strategy. Circle two addends to add first.
Write the sum. Then find the total sum. Then use a
different strategy and add again.

1.
$$
\begin{array}{r} 7 \\ 3 \\ +\,3 \\ \hline \end{array}\ \square
\qquad
\begin{array}{r} 7 \\ 3 \\ +\,3 \\ \hline \end{array}\ \square
$$

2.
$$
\begin{array}{r} 6 \\ 2 \\ +\,4 \\ \hline \end{array}\ \square
\qquad
\begin{array}{r} 6 \\ 2 \\ +\,4 \\ \hline \end{array}\ \square
$$

3.
$$
\begin{array}{r} 8 \\ 0 \\ +\,1 \\ \hline \end{array}\ \square
\qquad
\begin{array}{r} 8 \\ 0 \\ +\,1 \\ \hline \end{array}\ \square
$$

4.
$$
\begin{array}{r} 5 \\ 3 \\ +\,5 \\ \hline \end{array}\ \square
\qquad
\begin{array}{r} 5 \\ 3 \\ +\,5 \\ \hline \end{array}\ \square
$$

Problem Solving

Draw a picture. Complete the number
sentence.

5. Todd has 5 green paper clips. He has 2 blue
paper clips. He has 8 red paper clips.
How many paper clips does Todd have?

_____ + _____ + _____ = _____ paper clips

Choose the correct answer.

6. Zeb counts 2 black cars. He counts
   7 grey cars. He counts 1 red car.
   How many cars did Zeb count?

   ○ 8   ○ 10   ○ 9

7. Abby gave out paper party hats.
   She gave out 2 silver hats. She gave out
   4 pink hats. Then she gave out
   6 yellow hats. How many hats did
   Abby give out?

   ○ 12   ○ 6   ○ 10

8. **Multi-Step** Lana has 16 balloons. She has
   4 blue balloons. She has some green
   balloons. She has 5 purple balloons.
   How many green balloons does Lana
   have?

   ○ 11   ○ 9   ○ 7

9. What is the sum of $5 + 9 + 5$?

   ○ 13   ○ 19   ○ 10

TEKS Algebraic
Reasoning—1.5.F, 1.5.G
Also 1.3.C
MATHEMATICAL PROCESSES
1.1.B, 1.1.D, 1.1.E, 1.1.F

12.4 PROBLEM SOLVING • Use Addition Strategies

? Essential Question

How do you solve addition word problems by drawing a picture?

Unlock the Problem Real World

Megan put 8 fish in the tank. Tess put in 2 more fish. Then Bob put in 3 more fish. How many fish are in the tank now?

Read	Plan
What information am I given?	**What is my plan or strategy?**
Megan put in _____ fish.	I can _____
Tess put in _____ fish.	_____ .
Bob put in _____ fish.	

Solve

Show how you solve the problem.

____ ◯ ____ ◯ ____ ◯ ____   _____ fish

HOME CONNECTION • Your child will continue to use this chart to help him or her unlock the problem. In this lesson, your child used the strategy draw a picture to solve problems.

Draw a picture to solve.

- What information am I given?
- What is my plan or strategy?

I. Mark has 9 green toy cars.
He has 1 yellow toy car.
He also has 5 blue toy cars.
How many toy cars does he have?

_____ ◯ _____ ◯ _____ ◯ _____

____ toy cars

Math Talk
Mathematical Processes

Explain how make a ten helps you solve the problem.

Name _____

Draw a picture to solve.

2. Ava has 3 kites. Lexi has 3 kites. Fred has 5 kites. How many kites do they have?

____ ◯ ____ ◯ ____ ◯ ____   _____ kites

3. Al got 8 books at the library. Ryan got 7 books. Dee got 1 book. How many books do they have?

____ ◯ ____ ◯ ____ ◯ ____   _____ books

Problem Solving

4. **H.O.T.** There are 14 pencils. Haley has 6 pencils. Mac has 4 pencils. Sid has some pencils. How many pencils does Sid have?

_____ pencils

5. **H.O.T.** **Multi-Step** 12 marbles are in a bag. Shelly takes 3 marbles. Dan puts in 4. How many marbles are in the bag now?

_____ marbles

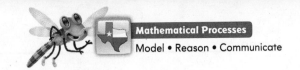

Mathematical Processes
Model • Reason • Communicate

Choose the correct answer.

6. There are 6 stones in the pail.
Lisa puts 5 more stones in the pail.
Then she puts 2 more stones in the pail.
How many stones are in the pail?

○ 13   ○ 11   ○ 7

7. Gerry, Dina, and Matt play a game.
Gerry scores 2 points. Dina scores 6 points.
Matt scores 2 points. How many points
do they score?

○ 8   ○ 12   ○ 10

8. **Connect** Jamal has 5 gray rocks, 4 blue rocks,
and 3 white rocks. How many rocks does
Jamal have?

○ 12   ○ 9   ○ 15

9. ⭐ **TEXAS Test Prep** Brooke has 7 pink shells,
8 white shells, and 3 brown shells.
How many shells does she have?

○ 10   ○ 18   ○ 15

TAKE HOME ACTIVITY • Have your child explain the
strategies he or she can use to add the numbers 7, 2, and 3.

TEKS Algebraic Reasoning—1.5.F, 1.5.G
Also 1.3.C
MATHEMATICAL PROCESSES 1.1.B, 1.1.D, 1.1.E, 1.1.F

Name _____

12.4 PROBLEM SOLVING • Use Addition Strategies

Draw a picture to solve.

1. Bart has 4 dogs. Kurt has 5 cats. Eve has 5 guinea pigs. How many pets to the friends have in all?

____ ◯ ____ ◯ ____ ◯ _____   _____ pets

2. Taneesha counted 7 birds on a feeder. The second day she counted 3 birds. The third day she counted 8 birds. How many birds did Taneesha count in all?

____ ◯ ____ ◯ ____ ◯ _____   _____ birds

3. Jan shared some stickers. Max took 5 stickers. Phil took 2 stickers. Trisha took 8 stickers. How many stickers were there?

____ ◯ ____ ◯ ____ ◯ _____   _____ stickers

Problem Solving Real World

4. There were 15 markers. 6 markers were blue. 4 markers were green. The rest were red. How many markers were red?

_____ red markers

Choose the correct answer.

5. Lena spins a spinner to see how many spaces to move in a game. First she spins a 7. Then she spins a 6. Then she spins a 3. How many spaces did Lena move?

○ 9   ○ 13   ○ 16

6. Tad, Mark, and Jill go fishing. Tad digs up 4 worms. Mark digs up 8 worms. Jill digs up 4 worms. How many worms do they dig up?

○ 16   ○ 12   ○ 15

7. **Multi-Step** Frank planted some seeds. He planted 7 bean seeds, 3 radish seeds, and 6 carrot seeds. Then he planted 2 sunflower seeds. How many seeds did Frank plant?

○ 16   ○ 18   ○ 10

8. Mel has 2 yellow stamps, 6 blue stamps, and 5 red stamps. How many stamps does Mel have?

○ 13   ○ 11   ○ 8

Module 12 Assessment

Concepts and Skills

Add. Change the order of
the addends. Add again. ◢ TEKS 1.5.F

1.

$$\begin{array}{r} 8 \\ + 4 \\ \hline \end{array}$$

☐
+ ☐
———
☐

2.

$$\begin{array}{r} 7 \\ + 9 \\ \hline \end{array}$$

☐
+ ☐
———
☐

Look at the 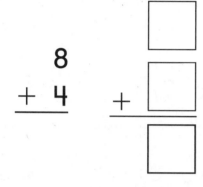. Complete the addition sentences
showing two ways to find the sum. ◢ TEKS 1.5.F, 1.5.G

3. $3 + 4 + 5 =$ _____

_____ + _____ = _____   _____ + _____ = _____

4. Write the number sentence.

Maria has 3 cats. Jim has 2 cats.
Cheryl has 5 cats. How many cats
do they have? ◢ TEKS 1.5.F, 1.5.G

_____ + _____ + _____ = _____ cats

© Houghton Mifflin Harcourt Publishing Company • Image Credits: ©PhotoDisc/Getty Images

Choose the correct answer.

5. Pete sends 4 letters.
   Then he sends 3 more letters.
   Then he sends 2 more letters.
   How many letters did Pete send? TEKS 1.5.F, 1.5.G

○ 7   ○ 6   ○ 9

---

6. Which shows the same addends
   in a different order? TEKS 1.5.F

$$7 + 6 = 13$$

○ $8 + 6 = 14$ │ ○ $6 + 7 = 13$ │ ○ $9 + 6 = 15$

---

7. What is the sum of $7 + 7 + 3$? TEKS 1.5.F, 1.5.G

○ 17   ○ 10   ○ 14

---

8. What is the sum of $10 + 0 + 10$? TEKS 1.5.F, 1.5.G

○ 10   ○ 20   ○ 2

Name _____

13.1
HANDS ON

Record Related Facts

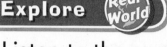
Essential Question

How do related facts help you find unknown numbers?

Explore Real World

Listen to the problem.
Model with . Draw .
Write the number sentence.

____ + ____ = ____   ____ − ____ = ____

FOR THE TEACHER • Read the following problem for the left box. Colin has 7 crackers. He gets 1 more cracker. How many crackers does Colin have now? Then read the following for the right box. Colin has 8 crackers. He gives one to Jacob. How many crackers does Colin have now?

Math Talk
Mathematical Processes

Explain how your model helps you write your number sentence.

Model and Draw

How can one model help you write four **related facts**?

$$4 + 5 = 9$$

$$9 - 5 = 4$$

$$5 + 4 = 9$$

$$9 - 4 = 5$$

Share and Show

MATH BOARD

Use . Add or subtract.
Complete the related facts.

1.

$$8 + \boxed{} = 15 \qquad 15 - 7 = \boxed{}$$

$$7 + 8 = \boxed{} \qquad \boxed{} - \boxed{} = \boxed{}$$

2.

$$\boxed{} + 9 = 14 \qquad 14 - \boxed{} = 5$$

$$9 + 5 = \boxed{} \qquad \boxed{} - \boxed{} = \boxed{}$$

3.

$$7 + \boxed{} = 13 \qquad 13 - 6 = \boxed{}$$

$$6 + 7 = \boxed{} \qquad \boxed{} - \boxed{} = \boxed{}$$

Problem Solving

Use 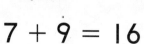. Add or subtract.
Complete the related facts.

4. ☐ + 8 = 13   13 − ☐ = 5

  8 + 5 = ☐   ☐ − ☐ = ☐

5.  H.O.T. Circle the number sentence
that has a mistake. Correct it to
complete the related facts.

  7 + 9 = 16   9 + 7 = 16

  16 + 9 = 7   16 − 7 = 9

  ____ ◯ ____ ◯ ____

6. H.O.T. Multi-Step Choose three numbers
to make related facts. Choose numbers between
0 and 18. Write your numbers. Write the
related facts.

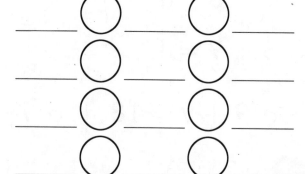

Mathematical Processes
Model • Reason • Communicate

Choose the correct answer.

7. Use to count.
Aunt Kay makes 6 instruments. Matt and Karen give her 3 more. Which completes the related facts?

$6 + 3 = 9$ $9 - 6 = 3$

$3 + 6 = 9$

○ $9 + 3 = 12$ | ○ $9 - 3 = 6$ | ○ $6 + 6 = 12$

8. **Analyze** Pete has 13 pencils. One day he uses 8 pencils. Another day he uses the rest. Which completes the related facts?

$13 - \boxed{} = 8$ $13 - 8 = \boxed{}$

$\boxed{} + 8 = 13$ $8 + \boxed{} = 13$

○ 6   ○ 8   ○ 5

9. ⭐ **TEXAS Test Prep** Which completes the related facts?

$9 + 8 = 17$ $17 - 8 = 9$

$8 + 9 = 17$

○ $9 + 9 = 18$ | ○ $9 - 6 = 3$ | ○ $17 - 9 = 8$

TAKE HOME ACTIVITY • Write an addition fact. Ask your child to write three other related facts.

TEKS Algebraic Reasoning—1.5.F, 1.5.G
MATHEMATICAL PROCESSES 1.1.C, 1.1.D, 1.1.F

13.1 HANDS ON   Record Related Facts

Add or subtract. Color to help you.
Complete the related facts.

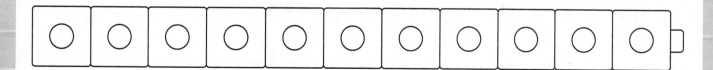

1. $\boxed{} + 5 = 11$ $11 - \boxed{} = 6$

   $5 + 6 = \boxed{}$ $\boxed{} - \boxed{} = \boxed{}$

Problem Solving Real World

Circle the number sentence that has a mistake.
Correct it to complete the related facts.

2. $6 + 8 = 14$ $8 - 6 = 14$

   $14 - 6 = 8$ $14 - 8 = 6$

   ___ ◯ ___ ◯ ___

Choose the correct answer.

3. Which completes the related facts?

$8 + 4 = 12$ $12 - 8 = 4$

$4 + 8 = 12$

○ $12 + 4 = 14$ | ○ $12 - 4 = 8$ | ○ $4 + 4 = 8$

4. Which completes the related facts?

$15 - 7 = \boxed{}$ $15 - \boxed{} = 7$

$7 + \boxed{} = 15$ $\boxed{} + 7 = 15$

○ 8   ○ 9   ○ 7

5. **Multi-Step** Write the related facts you can make with these 3 numbers: 5, 14, and 9.

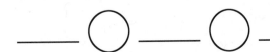

 **TEKS** Algebraic Reasoning—1.5.F, 1.5.G

MATHEMATICAL PROCESSES 1.1.F

13.2 Identify Related Facts

? Essential Question

How do you know if addition and subtraction facts are related?

Explore

Use ▪▪ to show $4 + 9 = 13$.

Draw ▪▪ to show a related subtraction fact.

Write the subtraction sentence.

___ ○ ___ ○ ___

Math Talk

Mathematical Processes

Explain why your subtraction sentence is related to $4 + 9 = 13$.

FOR THE TEACHER • Read the following problem. Brandon walks 9 miles in the morning. He walks 4 miles in the evening. How many miles does Brandon walk in a day? Write the related facts.

Use the pictures. What two facts can you write?

___ ◯ ___ ◯ ___

___ ◯ ___ ◯ ___

> These are related facts. If you know one of these facts, you also know the other fact.

Share and Show   MATH BOARD

Add and subtract.
Circle the related facts.

1. $6 + 4 =$ ___ $10 - 4 =$ ___	2. ___ $= 9 + 8$ ___ $= 17 - 8$	3. $9 + 5 =$ ___ $9 - 5 =$ ___
4. $8 + 7 =$ ___ $15 - 7 =$ ___	5. ___ $= 9 + 2$ ___ $= 9 - 2$	6. $6 + 3 =$ ___ $12 - 3 =$ ___
7. $4 + 8 =$ ___ $12 - 8 =$ ___	☑8. ___ $= 7 + 6$ ___ $= 13 - 6$	☑9. $9 + 9 =$ ___ $18 - 9 =$ ___

Problem Solving

10. Use these numbers to write the related facts. 8 9 17

___ ◯ ___ ◯ ___   ___ ◯ ___ ◯ ___

___ ◯ ___ ◯ ___   ___ ◯ ___ ◯ ___

11. **H.O.T.** Which number can **not** be used to write related number sentences? Explain.

_____

— —

H.O.T. **Multi-Step** Use the numbers to write related addition and subtraction sentences.

4 5 6 7 8 9 12 13 14

12. ___ ◯ ___ ◯ ___ | ___ ◯ ___ ◯ ___

13. ___ ◯ ___ ◯ ___ | ___ ◯ ___ ◯ ___

Daily Assessment Task

Choose the correct answer.

14. **Analyze** 11 elephants are washing themselves. Some elephants stop. 5 elephants keep washing themselves. Which fact is **not** related?

○ $11 - 6 = 5$ | ○ $5 + 6 = 11$ | ○ $6 - 5 = 1$

15. 9 elephants have their trunks up. 7 elephants do not have their trunks up. Which fact does **not** belong?

○ $9 + 7 = 16$ | ○ $16 - 6 = 10$ | ○ $16 - 9 = 7$

16. Jill has a garden. There are 4 roses. There are also 8 tulips. Which fact is **not** related?

○ $8 - 4 = 4$ | ○ $4 + 8 = 12$ | ○ $12 - 8 = 4$

17. ⭐ **TEXAS Test Prep** Which subtraction fact is related to $6 + 8 = 14$?

○ $14 - 7 = 7$ | ○ $14 - 8 = 6$ | ○ $14 - 9 = 5$

TAKE HOME ACTIVITY • Write 7, 9, 16, +, −, and = on separate slips of paper. Have your child use the slips of paper to show related facts.

13.2 Identify Related Facts

Add and subtract. Circle the related facts.

1. $8 + 5 =$ _____

   $13 - 5 =$ _____

2. $4 + 3 =$ _____

   $10 - 3 =$ _____

3. $9 + 4 =$ _____

   $9 - 4 =$ _____

Problem Solving

4. Which number can **not** be used to write related number sentences? Explain.

   5   7   9   14

   _____
   _____
   _____
   _____

Multi-Step Use the numbers to write related addition and subtraction sentences.

4   5   6   7   8   9   11   13   15

5. ____ ◯ ____ ◯ ____   ____ ◯ ____ ◯ ____

6. ____ ◯ ____ ◯ ____   ____ ◯ ____ ◯ ____

Choose the correct answer.

7. 13 squirrels are looking for nuts. Some squirrels stop. 6 squirrels keeping looking for nuts. Which fact is **not** related?

○ $13 - 7 = 6$ | ○ $7 - 6 = 1$ | ○ $6 + 7 = 13$

8. 8 cats are sleeping. 9 cats are not sleeping. Which fact does **not** belong?

○ $9 + 8 = 17$ | ○ $17 - 9 = 8$ | ○ $17 - 7 = 10$

9. Which subtraction fact is related to $8 + 3 = 11$?

○ $8 - 3 = 5$ | ○ $11 - 7 = 2$ | ○ $11 - 8 = 3$

10. **Multi-step** Mike has 5 soccer balls and 7 baseballs. Which number can **not** be used to write related number sentences with 5 and 7?

○ 8 | ○ 5 | ○ 12

TEKS Algebraic Reasoning—1.5.F, 1.5.G
MATHEMATICAL PROCESSES 1.1.F, 1.1.G

13.3 Use Addition to Check Subtraction

? **Essential Question**

How can you use addition to check subtraction?

Explore Real World

Draw and write to solve the problem.

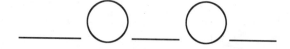

Math Talk

Mathematical Processes

Does Erin get all her books back? Use the number sentences to **explain** how you know.

FOR THE TEACHER • Read the problem. Erin has 11 books. I borrow 4 of them. How many books does Erin still have? Allow children time to solve, using the top workspace. Then read this part of the problem: I give 4 books back to Erin. How many books does Erin have now?

Model and Draw

Why can you use addition to check subtraction?

You subtract one part from the whole. The difference is the other part.

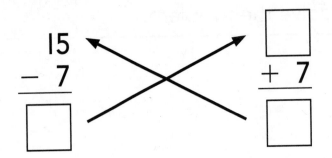

15
− 7
☐

☐
+ 7
☐

When you add the parts, you get the same whole.

Share and Show

 MATH BOARD

Subtract. Then add to check your answer.

1.

13
− 7
☐

☐
+ 7
☐

2.

14
− 5
☐

☐
+ 5
☐

✓3.

12
− 5
☐

☐
+ 5
☐

✓4.

17
− 9
☐

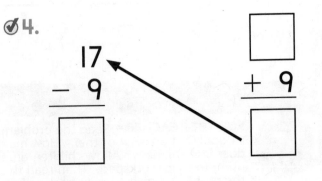

☐
+ 9
☐

Problem Solving

Subtract. Then add to check your answer.

5. $11 - 3 =$ ☐

    ☐ $+ 3 =$ ☐

6. $13 - 9 =$ ☐

    ☐ $+ 9 =$ ☐

7. $16 - 7 =$ ☐

    ☐ $+ 7 =$ ☐

8. $14 - 8 =$ ☐

    ☐ $+ 8 =$ ☐

9. **H.O.T.** Brianna has 13 sand dollars. Some sand dollars are broken. 5 sand dollars are not broken. Write number sentences about the sand dollars.

10. **H.O.T.** **Multi-Step** Subtract to solve. Then add to check your answer.

    Liam brings 15 cupcakes to the party. His friends eat all but 6 of them. How many cupcakes did they eat?

    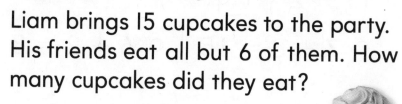

    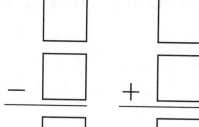

    _____ cupcakes

Mathematical Processes
Model • Reason • Communicate

Choose the correct answer.

11. **Analyze** 12 rabbits are in the pen. 3 rabbits are given away. 9 rabbits are left. Which addition sentence can you use to check the subtraction?

○ $8 + 3 = 11$ ○ $3 + 9 = 12$ ○ $12 + 3 = 15$

12. There are 13 ladybugs on a plant. Then 7 fly away. 6 ladybugs are left. Which fact can you use to check the subtraction?

○ $6 + 7 = 13$ ○ $13 - 8 = 5$ ○ $7 - 6 = 1$

13. **Multi-Step** There are 15 people on a bus. 8 people get off. How many people are left? Which addition sentence can you use to check the subtraction?

○ $15 + 8 = 23$ ○ $8 + 9 = 17$ ○ $7 + 8 = 15$

14. ⭐ **TEXAS Test Prep** Which addition sentence can you use to check the subtraction?

$$11 - 2 = \boxed{}$$

○ $9 + 2 = 11$ ○ $7 + 8 = 15$ ○ $6 + 2 = 8$

TAKE HOME ACTIVITY • Write $11 - 7 = \square$ on a sheet of paper. Ask your child to find the difference and then write an addition sentence he or she can use to check the subtraction.

13.3 Use Addition to Check Subtraction

Subtract. Then add to check your answer.

1. $13 - 8 = \boxed{}$

   $\boxed{} + 8 = \boxed{}$

2. $16 - 9 = \boxed{}$

   $\boxed{} + 9 = \boxed{}$

3. $11 - 6 = \boxed{}$

   $\boxed{} + 6 = \boxed{}$

4. $17 - 8 = \boxed{}$

   $\boxed{} + 8 = \boxed{}$

Problem Solving Real World

5. Marty has 14 stickers. Some stickers are torn. 8 stickers are not torn. Write number sentences about the stickers.

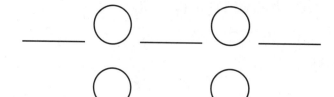

Choose the correct answer.

6. 14 flowers are on a bush. Mike picks 6 flowers. 8 flowers are left on the bush. Which addition sentence can you use to check the subtraction?

○ $6 + 8 = 14$ | ○ $7 + 6 = 13$ | ○ $14 + 4 = 18$

7. There are 17 children on a trip to the zoo. 9 children go to see the monkeys. The rest go to see the snakes.

$17 - 9 = \square$

Which fact can you use to check the subtraction?

$$\circ \quad \begin{array}{r} 9 \\ -\ 8 \\ \hline 1 \end{array} \qquad \circ \quad \begin{array}{r} 16 \\ -\ 9 \\ \hline 7 \end{array} \qquad \circ \quad \begin{array}{r} 8 \\ +\ 9 \\ \hline 17 \end{array}$$

8. Which addition sentence can you use to check the subtraction?

$12 - 5 = \square$

○ $6 + 6 = 12$ | ○ $7 + 5 = 12$ | ○ $9 + 5 = 14$

9. **Multi-step** There are 15 children on the playground. 6 children go inside. How many children are left? Which addition sentence can you use to check the subtraction?

○ $15 + 6 = 21$ | ○ $6 + 9 = 15$ | ○ $6 + 8 = 14$

TEKS Algebraic Reasoning—1.5.F, 1.5.G

MATHEMATICAL PROCESSES
1.1.C, 1.1.D, 1.1.F

13.4 Unknown Numbers

HANDS ON ALGEBRA

? Essential Question

How can you use a known part to find an unknown number?

Explore Real World

 Hands On

Listen to the problem. Use to show the story. Draw to show your work.

Math Talk
Mathematical Processes

How many toy cars are blue? **Explain** how you got your answer.

 FOR THE TEACHER • Read the problem. Calvin has 7 toy cars that are red. He has some blue toy cars. He has 10 toy cars. How many blue toy cars does Calvin have?

What are the unknown numbers?

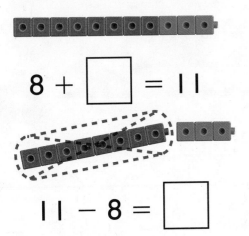

$8 + \boxed{} = 11$

$11 - 8 = \boxed{}$

Use what you know about related facts to find the unknown parts.

Share and Show

Use to find the unknown numbers.
Write the numbers.

1. $8 + \boxed{} = 15$

   $15 - 8 = \boxed{}$

2. $13 = 9 + \boxed{}$

   $\boxed{} = 13 - 9$

3. $5 + \boxed{} = 14$

   $14 - 5 = \boxed{}$

4. $14 = 6 + \boxed{}$

   $\boxed{} = 14 - 6$

5. $9 + \boxed{} = 16$

   $16 - 9 = \boxed{}$

6. $17 = 8 + \boxed{}$

   $\boxed{} = 17 - 8$

Name _____

Problem Solving

Write the unknown numbers.
Use  if you need to.

7. $7 + \boxed{} = 15$

   $15 - 7 = \boxed{}$

8. $5 + \boxed{} = 11$

   $11 - 5 = \boxed{}$

9. $\boxed{} + 10 = 20$

   $20 - 10 = \boxed{}$

10. $\boxed{} + 9 = 16$

   $16 - 9 = \boxed{}$

11. **H.O.T.** Solve.

Rick has 10 party hats.
He needs 19 hats for his party.
How many more party hats
does Rick need?

_____ party hats

12. **H.O.T.** **Multi-Step** Solve.
Use 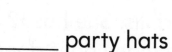 if you need to.

There were 15 children at the park.
Some children went home.
Then 4 more children came to the park.
Now there are 13 children at the park.
How many children went home?   _____ children

Mathematical Processes
Model • Reason • Communicate

Use , . Choose the correct answer.

13. Analyze 14 cars are at the starting line. 10 cars cross the finish line. How many cars did not cross the finish line?

$$10 + \boxed{} = 14$$

○ 4   ○ 9   ○ 5

14. Nick has 3 blue cubes in his hand. The cubes on his desk are yellow. He has 12 cubes. How many yellow cubes does Nick have?

$$3 + \boxed{} = 12 \qquad 12 - \boxed{} = 3$$

○ 6   ○ 9   ○ 4

15. Multi-Step Tori counts the toys in her toy box. She has 3 bears and 3 cars. The rest are dolls. She has 12 toys in her toy box. How many dolls does Tori have?

○ 9   ○ 5   ○ 6

16. ⭐ **TEXAS Test Prep** What is the unknown number?

$$9 + \boxed{} = 18$$

○ 8   ○ 9   ○ 11

TAKE HOME ACTIVITY • Have your child explain how using subtraction can help him or her find the unknown number in 7 + □ = 16.

Homework and Practice

Name _____

TEKS Algebraic Reasoning—1.5.F, 1.5.G
MATHEMATICAL PROCESSES 1.1.C, 1.1.D, 1.1.F

13.4 Unknown Numbers

HANDS ON ALGEBRA

Write the unknown numbers.
Draw ● if you need to.

1. $9 + \boxed{} = 18$

   $18 - 9 = \boxed{}$

2. $7 + \boxed{} = 15$

   $15 - 7 = \boxed{}$

3. $12 = 8 + \boxed{}$

   $\boxed{} = 12 - 8$

4. $\boxed{} + 6 = 15$

   $15 - 6 = \boxed{}$

Problem Solving

5. Mr. Brown has 7 sleeping bags.
   He has 16 campers. How many
   more sleeping bags does
   Mr. Brown need?

_____ sleeping bags

Choose the correct answer.

6. 14 children are walking to raise money.
8 children finish the walk. How many
children did not finish the walk?

$$8 + \boxed{} = 14$$

○ 4   ○ 7   ○ 6

7. Jasmine has 6 red pencils in her pencil case.
The pencils in her hand are blue. She has
13 pencils. How many blue pencils does
Jasmine have?

$$6 + \boxed{} = 13 \qquad 13 - \boxed{} = 6$$

○ 6   ○ 1   ○ 7

8. What is the unknown number?

$$\boxed{} + 8 = 16$$

○ 8   ○ 9   ○ 7

9. **Multi-step** Sam has 17 shirts in
his drawer. He has 5 red shirts and
4 green shirts. The rest of his shirts
are blue. How many blue shirts
does Sam have?

○ 9   ○ 8   ○ 10

TEKS Algebraic Reasoning—1.5.F, 1.5.G
MATHEMATICAL PROCESSES 1.1.D, 1.1.F

13.5 Use Related Facts

ALGEBRA

Essential Question How can you use a related fact to find an unknown number?

Explore

What number can you add to 8 to get 10?
Draw a picture to solve.
Write the unknown number.

$$8 + \boxed{} = 10$$

Math Talk

Mathematical Processes

Describe how to solve this problem using cubes.

FOR THE TEACHER • Read the following problem. Dean has number cards for 8 and 10. What number card would Dean need to add to 8 to get 10?

Model and Draw

You can use an addition fact to find a related subtraction fact.

Find $10 - 3$.

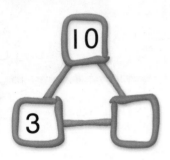

$3 + \rule{1.5cm}{0.4pt} = 10$

$10 - 3 = \rule{1.5cm}{0.4pt}$

I know that
$3 + 7 = 10$, so
$10 - 3 = 7$.

Share and Show MATH BOARD

Write the unknown numbers.

1. Find $14 - 8$.

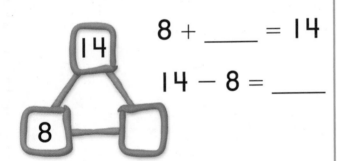

$8 + \rule{1.5cm}{0.4pt} = 14$

$14 - 8 = \rule{1.5cm}{0.4pt}$

2. Find $17 - 8$.

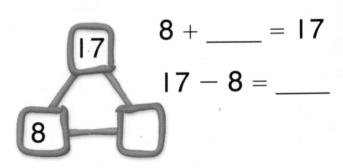

$8 + \rule{1.5cm}{0.4pt} = 17$

$17 - 8 = \rule{1.5cm}{0.4pt}$

3. Find $11 - 6$.

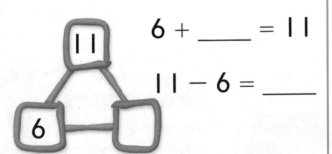

$6 + \rule{1.5cm}{0.4pt} = 11$

$11 - 6 = \rule{1.5cm}{0.4pt}$

4. Find $15 - 9$.

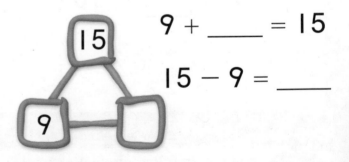

$9 + \rule{1.5cm}{0.4pt} = 15$

$15 - 9 = \rule{1.5cm}{0.4pt}$

Name _____

Problem Solving

Write the unknown numbers.

5. Find 20 − 10.

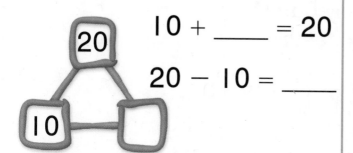

10 + ____ = 20

20 − 10 = ____

6. Find 13 − 4.

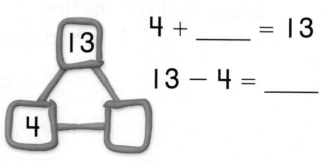

4 + ____ = 13

13 − 4 = ____

7. H.O.T.

 + ★ = ▮   ▮ − ____ = ____

H.O.T. **Multi-Step** Write an addition sentence to help you find the difference. Then write the related subtraction sentence to solve.

8. Find 11 − 5.

____ + ____ = ____

____ − ____ = ____

9. Find 13 − 6.

____ = ____ + ____

____ = ____ − ____

Choose the correct answer.

10. 15 baby bears brush their teeth before going to bed. 8 baby bears still need to brush their teeth. How many baby bears have already brushed their teeth?

$$15 - 8 = \square \qquad 8 + \square = 15$$

○ 7   ○ 6   ○ 1

11. **Analyze** Hanna has 11 baseball cards. She gives 5 away. She wants to know how many are left. Which number sentence will help you find the missing number?

○ $11 + 5 = 16$ | ○ $5 + 6 = 11$ | ○ $6 - 5 = 1$

12. John has 10 books. He reads some books. He has 6 books left to read. Which shows the unknown number of books John has read?

○ $10 - \square = 6$ | ○ $10 - \square = 2$ | ○ $4 + \square = 8$

13. ⭐ **TEXAS Test Prep** Which addition fact helps you solve $17 - 8$?

○ $8 + 7 = 15$ | ○ $9 + 8 = 17$ | ○ $9 + 9 = 18$

TAKE HOME ACTIVITY • Give your child 5 small objects, such as paper clips. Then ask your child how many more objects he or she would need to have 12.

13.5 Use Related Facts

ALGEBRA

Write the unknown numbers.

1. Find $16 - 7$.

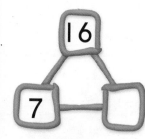

$7 + \underline{\quad} = 16$

$16 - 7 = \underline{\quad}$

2. Find $12 - 5$.

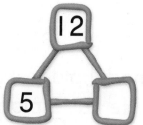

$5 + \underline{\quad} = 12$

$12 - 5 = \underline{\quad}$

3. Find $14 - 6$.

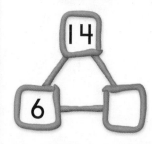

$6 + \underline{\quad} = 14$

$14 - 6 = \underline{\quad}$

4. Find $13 - 8$.

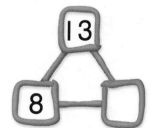

$8 + \underline{\quad} = 13$

$13 - 8 = \underline{\quad}$

Problem Solving

Multi-Step Write an addition sentence to help you find the difference. Then write the related subtraction sentence to solve.

5. Find $17 - 9$.

$\underline{\quad} + \underline{\quad} = \underline{\quad}$

$\underline{\quad} - \underline{\quad} = \underline{\quad}$

6. Find $15 - 6$.

$\underline{\quad} = \underline{\quad} + \underline{\quad}$

$\underline{\quad} = \underline{\quad} - \underline{\quad}$

Choose the correct answer.

7. Tina washes 16 dishes after dinner. She still needs to wash 9 of the dishes. How many dishes has Tina already washed?

$$16 - 9 = \boxed{} \qquad 9 + \boxed{} = 16$$

○ 7　　　　　　　○ 9　　　　　　　○ 8

8. Nate has 12 model planes. He paints some planes. He has 5 planes left to paint. Which shows how many planes Nate has left to paint?

○ $12 - \boxed{} = 8$

○ $5 + \boxed{} = 7$

○ $12 - \boxed{} = 5$

9. Which addition fact helps you solve 15 − 7?

○ $7 + 9 = 16$　│　○ $7 + 8 = 15$　│　○ $6 + 9 = 15$

10. Mark wants to find 13 − 5. Which shows the related subtraction sentence?

○ $13 - 8 = 5$

○ $13 - 9 = 4$

○ $13 - 6 = 7$

Name _____

13.6 Expressions
ALGEBRA

? Essential Question

How can you decide if the expressions on each side of the equal sign have the same value?

Explore

Color the cards that have the same value.

2 + 6	12 − 6	6 + 1
13 − 6	15 − 8	10 + 6
3 + 4	4 + 3	5 + 7
5 + 2	11 − 2	16 − 9

Math Talk
Mathematical Processes

Explain why you can use two of the cards you color and an equal sign to show the same value.

FOR THE TEACHER • Have children color the cards that have the same value.

Model and Draw

The equal sign means that both sides have the same value.

Write a number to show expressions with the same value.

4 + 5 = 5 + 5 does **not** show the same values on each side of the equal sign.

$$4 + 5 = \underline{} + 4$$

Share and Show

THINK
Are both sides equal?

Which expressions show equal values? Circle your answer.
Which expressions do not show equal values? Cross out your answer.

1.

$$9 - 2 = 8 - 1$$

$$1 + 2 = 3 - 2$$

2.

$$4 + 1 = 5 + 2$$

$$6 - 6 = 7 - 7$$

3.

$$7 + 2 = 6 + 3$$

$$8 - 2 = 6 + 4$$

4.

$$5 - 4 = 4 - 3$$

$$7 + 3 = 1 + 0$$

Problem Solving

Which expressions show equal values?
Circle your answers. Which expressions do not
show equal values? Cross out your answers.

5.

| $1 + 9 = 9 - 1$ | $8 + 1 = 2 + 7$ | $10 + 9 = 12 + 7$ |

6.

| $7 + 1 = 5 + 3$ | $8 + 5 = 5 + 8$ | $6 + 2 = 4 + 4$ |

7.

| $9 + 7 = 8 + 8$ | $16 - 9 = 9 + 7$ | $9 - 7 = 7 + 9$ |

8.

| $12 - 3 = 9 - 0$ | $11 + 0 = 1 + 10$ | $10 - 0 = 8 - 2$ |

9. **H.O.T.** Write numbers to show expressions
of equal value.

____ + ____ = ____ + ____

10. **H.O.T.** **Multi-Step** Emily has 2 books. Then
she gets 8 more books. Justin has 15 books.
He gives away 5 books. Do they have an
equal amount of books? Write the expressions
to show how you solved the problem.

____ ◯ ____ ◯ ____ ◯ ____

Daily Assessment Task

Choose the correct answer.

11. Analyze The camp has 3 yellow tents and 2 red tents. Which expression shows the same value?

○ $5 - 2$ ○ $4 + 1$ ○ $5 + 1$

---

12. Which expressions show the same value?

○ $6 + 2 = 11 - 3$
○ $8 - 1 = 8 + 1$
○ $5 + 7 = 13 - 4$

---

13. Danielle has 4 red balls and 6 yellow balls. Which expression shows the same value?

○ $5 + 7$
○ $8 + 2$
○ $13 - 6$

14. ⭐ **TEXAS Test Prep** Which number would make expressions of equal value?

$$10 - 3 = 2 + \underline{\quad}$$

○ 5 ○ 6 ○ 7

TAKE HOME ACTIVITY • Write $10 - 3 = 7 - 3$ and $10 + 0 = 7 + 3$ on a sheet of paper. Ask your child to explain which expressions show the same value.

TEKS Algebraic Reasoning—1.5.E
MATHEMATICAL PROCESSES 1.1.C, 1.1.D, 1.1.F

Name _____

13.6 ALGEBRA Expressions

Which expressions show equal values? Circle your answer. Which expressions do not show equal values? Cross out your answer.

1.		
$7 + 4 = 5 + 6$	$13 - 5 = 8 + 5$	$10 + 0 = 9 + 1$

2.		
$14 - 6 = 4 + 4$	$8 + 4 = 3 + 9$	$8 + 7 = 6 + 9$

3.		
$17 - 9 = 3 + 4$	$2 + 7 = 13 - 4$	$8 + 3 = 8 - 3$

Problem Solving Real World

4. **Multi-Step** Daryl has 7 movies. Then he gets 5 more movies. Serena has 18 movies. She gives away 6 movies. Do they have an equal number of movies? Write the expressions to show how you solved the problem.

____ ◯ ____ ◯ ____ ◯

Choose the correct answer.

5. Kevin has 5 blue balloons and 4 yellow balloons. Which expression shows the same value?

  ○ 3 + 6   ○ 9 − 4   ○ 9 + 1

6. Which expressions show the same value?

  ○ 4 + 9 = 13 − 9

  ○ 15 − 7 = 6 + 2

  ○ 14 − 8 = 6 + 9

7. Which number would make expressions of equal value?

  $$13 - 4 = 7 + \underline{\hspace{1cm}}$$

  ○ 2

  ○ 11

  ○ 3

8. Steve has 14 pictures. He gives away 6. Which expressions show the same value?

  ○ 5 + 3 = 4 + 6

  ○ 5 − 3 = 14 − 6

  ○ 5 + 3 = 14 − 6

Name _____

 Module 13 Assessment

1. Complete the **related facts**. (p. 460)

$9 + \boxed{} = 15$ $\qquad$ $15 - \boxed{} = 9$

$6 + \boxed{} = 15$ $\qquad$ $15 - \boxed{} = 6$

Concepts and Skills

2. Complete the related facts. ◆ TEKS 1.5.F, 1.5.G

$\boxed{} + 8 = 17$ $\qquad$ $17 - \boxed{} = 9$

$8 + 9 = \boxed{}$ $\qquad$ $\boxed{} - \boxed{} = \boxed{}$

3. Subtract. Then add to check your answer. ◆ TEKS 1.5.F, 1.5.G

$$\begin{array}{r} 16 \\ -\ 9 \\ \hline \boxed{} \end{array} \qquad\qquad \begin{array}{r} 7 \\ +\ 9 \\ \hline \boxed{} \end{array}$$

4. Write the unknown numbers. Explain how you got your answer. ◆ TEKS 1.5.F, 1.5.G

$\boxed{} + 5 = 13$ $\qquad$ $13 - 5 = \boxed{}$

Choose the correct answer.

5. Which number will show expressions of the
   same value? ★ TEKS 1.5.E

   $$0 + 9 = \boxed{} - 9$$

   ○ 18   ○ 9   ○ 0

6. Which is the related fact for
   $9 + 5 = 14$? ★ TEKS 1.5.F, 1.5.G

   ○ $14 - 5 = 9$
   ○ $9 - 5 = 4$
   ○ $14 - 4 = 10$

7. Which addition fact can you use to check the
   subtraction for $15 - 6 = $ _____ ? ★ TEKS 1.5.F, 1.5.G

   ○ $5 + $ _____ $= 15$
   ○ $6 + $ _____ $= 15$
   ○ $10 + $ _____ $= 15$

8. Which number completes the related fact?

   $9 + 9 = $ _____ and _____ $- 9 = 9$ ★ TEKS 1.5.F, 1.5.G

   ○ 19   ○ 16   ○ 18

9. Which expressions have an equal value? ★ TEKS 1.5.E

   ○ $5 + 12 = 12 - 5$
   ○ $2 + 10 = 7 + 5$
   ○ $18 - 7 = 11 + 7$

Mifflin Harcourt Publishing Company

Unit 3 Assessment

Vocabulary

Write to complete the **related facts**. (p. 460)

1. $9 + 7 = 16$ $16 - 7 = 9$

    $7 + 9 = 16$ ___ ◯ ___ ◯ ___

Concepts and Skills

Complete the model and the number sentence.

2. Alli has 10 grapes.
    She eats 5 grapes.
    How many grapes does
    she still have? ⬇ TEKS 1.5.D

5	___

10

$10 - 5 =$ ___

Count forward by ones. Write the numbers. ⬇ TEKS 1.5.A

3. 35, 36, _____, _____, _____, _____

Count backward by ones. Write the numbers. ⬇ TEKS 1.5.A

4. 96, 95, _____, _____, _____, _____

5. There are 15 balloons.
8 balloons are green.
The rest are purple.
How many balloons
are purple? ⬇ TEKS 1.5.D

○ 7

○ 15

○ 8

6. Which is the related fact for
$9 + 7 = 16$? ⬇ TEKS 1.5.F, 1.5.G

○ $9 - 7 = 2$

○ $16 - 7 = 9$

○ $17 - 9 = 8$

7. Which shows the same addends in
a different order? ⬇ TEKS 1.5.F

$$5 + 9 = 14$$

○ $5 + 8 = 13$

○ $9 + 4 = 13$

○ $9 + 5 = 14$

8. Which addition fact can you use
to check the subtraction for

$13 - 8 = $ _____? ⬇ TEKS 1.5.F, 1.5.G

○ $10 + $ _____ $= 13$

○ $13 + $ _____ $= 13$

○ $8 + $ _____ $= 13$

9. There are 3 turtles in the pond.
Some more turtles join them.
Now there are 9 turtles in the
pond. How many turtles joined
them? ⬇ TEKS 1.5.D

○ 11

○ 6

○ 12

Choose the correct answer.

10. There are 12 deer in the woods. Seven of the deer run away. Five deer are left in the woods. Which fact can you use to check the subtraction? TEKS 1.5.F, 1.5.G

- ○ $6 + 9 = 15$
- ○ $12 + 5 = 17$
- ○ $5 + 7 = 12$

11. Which is the unknown number?
TEKS 1.5.F, 1.5.G

____ $+ 8 = 17$

$17 - 8 =$ ____

- ○ 17
- ○ 9
- ○ 3

12. Tamara has 3 dolls. Kelly has 7 dolls. How many fewer dolls does Tamara have than Kelly? TEKS 1.5.D

- ○ 3
- ○ 10
- ○ 4

13. Which number shows expressions of equal value? TEKS 1.5.E

$6 + 3 =$ ____ $- 2$

- ○ 10
- ○ 6
- ○ 11

14. Amy has 7 gifts. Then she gets 2 more gifts. Then she gets 3 more gifts. How many gifts does Amy have?
TEKS 1.5.F

- ○ 12
- ○ 9
- ○ 10

TEXAS Test Prep

15. Which number is ten less than 57? 🔽 TEKS 1.5.C

- ○ 75
- ○ 47
- ○ 40

16. Use 🔲, ⬤, or real objects to solve.

There are 15 children in the park.

_____ children are playing ball.

_____ children are not playing ball.

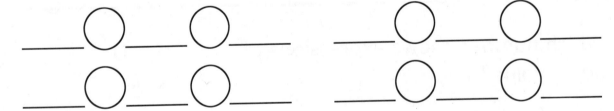

- What information am I given?
- What is my plan or strategy?
- How can I solve?
- How can I check my answer?

- Write numbers to complete the story problem.

- Explain how you chose the numbers.

- Write the related facts for the story problem.

_____ ◯ _____ ◯ _____   _____ ◯ _____ ◯ _____

_____ ◯ _____ ◯ _____   _____ ◯ _____ ◯ _____

- Explain how to use addition to check subtraction. 🔽 TEKS 1.3.D, 1.3.E, 1.5.G
  Justify. Explain why your answer is reasonable.

Geometry and Measurement

Name _____

Alike and Different

Circle the objects that are alike.

1.

2.

Longer and Shorter

Circle the longer object.
Draw a line under the shorter object.

3.

4.

Identify Two-Dimensional Shapes

Color each square blue. Color each
rectangle yellow. Color each circle red.

5.

 FAMILY NOTE: This page checks your child's understanding of
important skills needed for success in Unit 4.

GO DIGITAL Assessment Options:
Soar to Success Math

Review Words

circle
cone
cube
cylinder
sphere
square
triangle

Visualize It

Write review words to name the solids.

sphere
_____

_____

three-dimensional
solids

_____

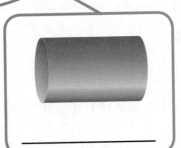

_____

Understand Vocabulary

Write the number of each shape.

1. ____ circles

2. ____ squares

3. ____ triangles

GO
DIGITAL
• Interactive Student Edition
• Multimedia eGlossary

City Figures

written by J. D. McDonnell

illustrated by Judith Moffatt

This Take-Home Book belongs to

_____

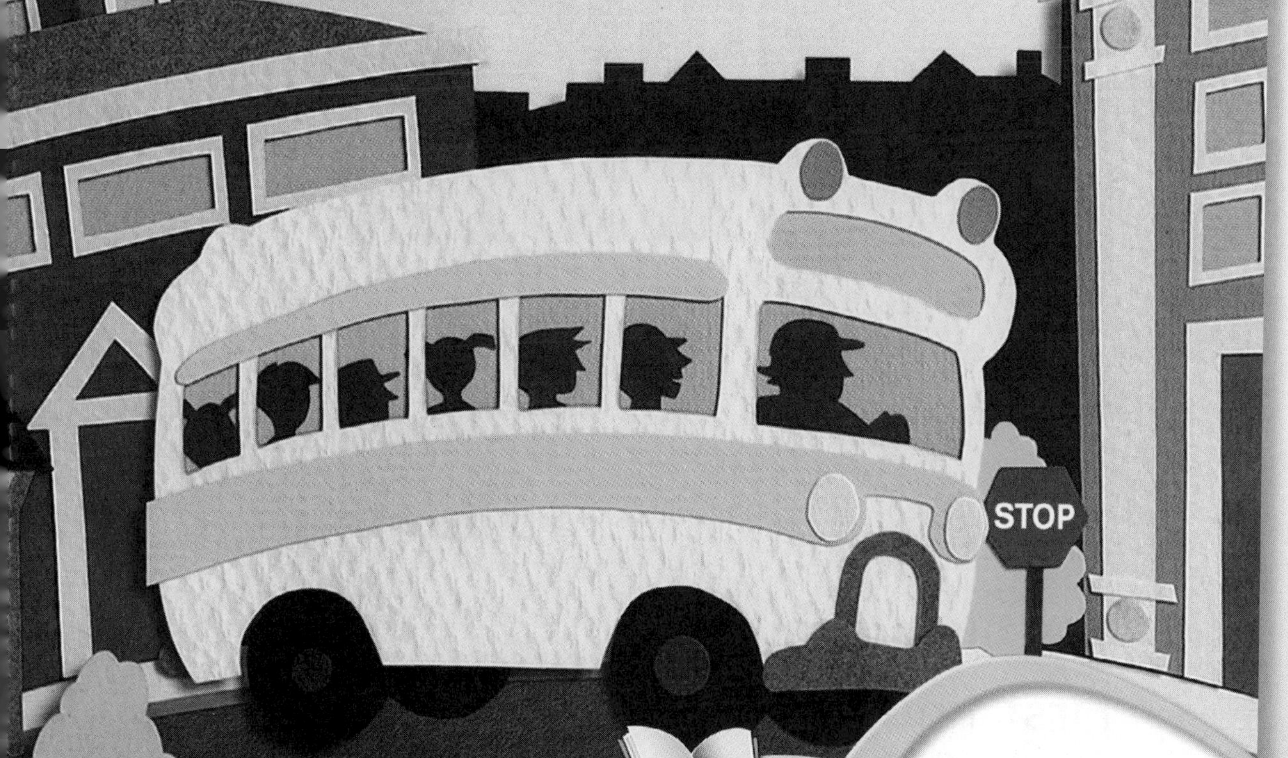

STOP

Reading and Writing Math

This take-home book will help you preview two-dimensional figures.

MATHEMATICAL PROCESSES 1.1.A, 1.1.D

We're on our way to school.
We play a shape hunt. It's so cool!
First find a square with equal sides,
1, 2, 3, 4.
Look! I spy one at the shoe store!

Find other figures shaped like a square.

The next figure that we look for
Is the circle. It's so round.
Finding them is no chore,
For circles here abound.

Find figures shaped like a circle.

Triangles are now next.
This figure has sides, 1, 2, 3.
Now don't be perplexed.
There are many here to see!

Find figures shaped like a triangle.

We're almost to our school,
As through the streets we wind.
Wait! We made a simple game rule
4 figures we must find!

Find figures shaped like a rectangle.

We're now here in our classroom,
At our desks, and in our chairs.
It was fun finding triangles,
circles, rectangles and squares.

Find and name these figures in
our classroom.

Our game has ended, but this
book is not done.
Draw a city picture. Include all
4 figures just for fun!

Write about the Math

Write Math Look at these shapes. Draw a picture, and write your own story about shapes in your classroom or outside.

Vocabulary Review

circle	shape
square	round
rectangle	sides
triangle	

_____

- -

_____

- -

_____

- -

_____

- -

_____

- -

_____

The Shape of Things

Look at the shapes in the picture.

1. How many squares can you find?

   _____ squares

2. How many circles can you find?

   _____ circles

3. How many rectangles can you find?

   _____ rectangles

4. How many triangles can you find?

   _____ triangles

MATH BOARD Draw a building you might see in the city. Use all 4 shapes. Have a classmate find and name each shape.

Name _____

14.1 Classify and Sort Two-Dimensional Shapes

? Essential Question

How can you use attributes to classify and sort two-dimensional shapes?

Explore  Hands On

Draw to sort the shapes.
Write the sorting rule.

_____ | _____
- - - - - - - - - - - - - - - - | - - - - - - - - - - - - - - - - -

Math Talk
Mathematical Processes

Are there shapes that did not go in your groups? **Explain.**

FOR THE TEACHER • Read the following aloud. Devon wants to sort these shapes to show a group of triangles and a group of rectangles. Draw and write to show how Devon sorts the shapes.

© Houghton Mifflin Harcourt Publishing Company

Model and Draw

Here are some ways to classify and sort two-dimensional shapes.

> A **square** is a special kind of rectangle.

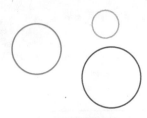 **curved** and closed shapes

closed shapes with ____ **sides**

closed shapes with ____ **vertices**

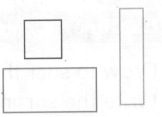

circles

triangles

rectangles

Share and Show

MATH BOARD

> **THINK**
> Vertices (corners) are where the sides meet.

Read the sorting rule. Circle the shapes that follow the rule.

1. 4 vertices (corners)

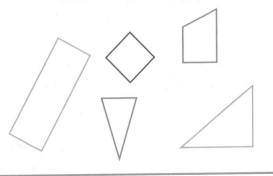

2. **not** curved

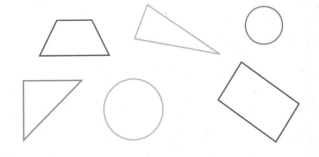

✓3 triangles

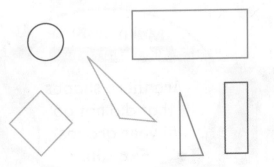

✓4. more than 3 sides

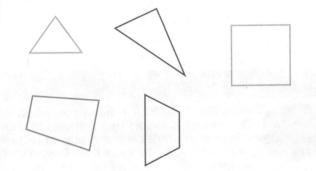

514 five hundred fourteen

Problem Solving

Circle the special rectangles in Exercise 6.

5. Color the shapes that are circles.

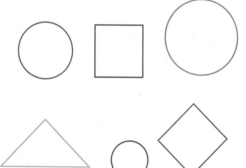

6. Color the squares red. Color other rectangles blue.

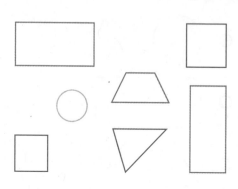

H.O.T. Draw 2 different two-dimensional shapes that follow both parts of the sorting rule.

7. 3 sides and 3 vertices (corners)

8. 2 sides are long and 2 sides are short

9. **H.O.T. Multi-Step** Write sorting rules to show two different ways to sort some of these shapes. Then color the shapes that follow one of your rules.

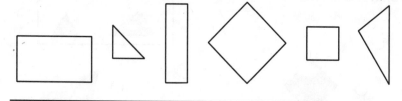

_____

- -

_____

Daily Assessment Task

Mathematical Processes
Model • Reason • Communicate

Choose the correct answer.

10. Analyze Which shape is a rectangle?

○ ⬭

○ ▭

○ △

11. Multi-Step Circle the triangles. Then circle the sorting rule you used.

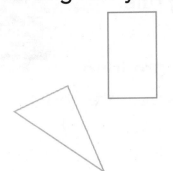

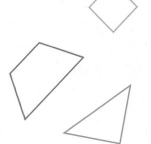

3 sides   **curved**   **4 sides**

12. ⭐ **TEXAS Test Prep** Which shape would **not** be sorted into this group?

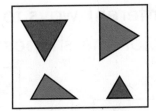

○   ○ ◆   ○ ◣

 TAKE HOME ACTIVITY • Gather some household objects such as photos, coins, and napkins. Ask your child to sort them by shape.

516 five hundred sixteen

Homework and Practice

Name _____

14.1 Classify and Sort Two-Dimensional Shapes

Read the sorting rule. Circle the shapes that follow the rule.

1. more than 3 sides

2. circles

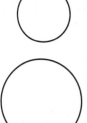

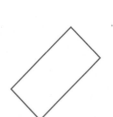

Problem Solving Real World

Draw 2 different two-dimensional shapes that follow both parts of the sorting rule.

3. 4 sides are the same length

---

4. Multi-Step Write sorting rules to show two different ways to sort some of these shapes.

_____

_ _

_____

Choose the correct answer.

5. Which shape is **not** curved?

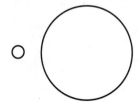 ○   ○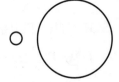

6. Which shape is a special rectangle?

○ 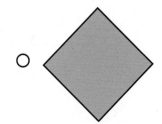 ○ 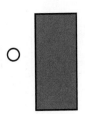 ○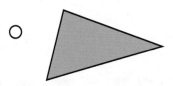

7. **Multi-Step** Kara is sorting shapes. Read the labels. Circle the shapes that belong in each group.

squares	**rectangles**

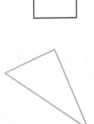   

518 five hundred eighteen

Name _____

Attributes of Two-Dimensional Shapes

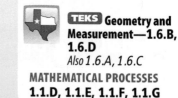
TEKS Geometry and Measurement—1.6.B, 1.6.D
Also 1.6.A, 1.6.C
MATHEMATICAL PROCESSES
1.1.D, 1.1.E, 1.1.F, 1.1.G

 Essential Question

What attributes can you use to describe two-dimensional shapes?

Explore

Use two-dimensional shapes. Sort them into two groups. Draw to show your work.

curved	straight

Math Talk
Mathematical Processes

Explain how you sorted the shapes into two groups. Name the shapes in each group.

 FOR THE TEACHER • Have children sort two-dimensional shapes into groups that are curved and straight. Have them draw the shapes to show how they sorted.

Model and Draw

Some shapes have straight sides and vertices.

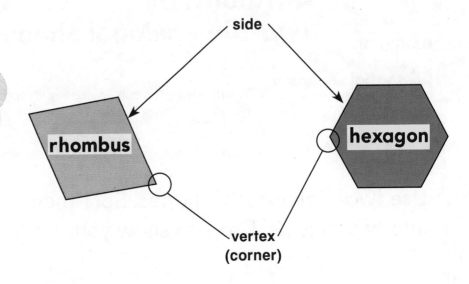

side

rhombus

hexagon

vertex
(corner)

Share and Show

MATH BOARD

Use two-dimensional shapes. Draw and write to complete the chart.

	Shape	Draw the shape.	Number of Straight Sides	Number of Vertices (Corners)
1.	hexagon			
2.	rectangle			
⊘3.	square			
4.	rhombus			
⊘5.	triangle			

Name _____

Use  to trace each straight side.

Use  to circle each vertex (corner).

Write the number of sides and vertices (corners).

6.

_____ sides

_____ vertices

7.

_____ sides

_____ vertices

8. Circle the rhombus.

9. Color the hexagon red.

H.O.T. Draw a picture to solve.

10. I am a shape with 3 straight sides and 3 vertices.

11. I am a shape with 4 straight sides that are the same length and 4 vertices.

12. **H.O.T.** **Multi-Step** Draw two different shapes that each have only 4 vertices.

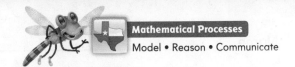

Mathematical Processes
Model • Reason • Communicate

Choose the correct answer.

13. Analyze Tom draws a closed shape with only a curved surface. Which shape does he draw?

○ circle

○ hexagon

○ rectangle

14. Use words from the box. Write the shape names. Write the number of sides and vertices (corners).

rhombus
rectangle
hexagon

_____

- - - - - - - - - - - - - - - - -

_____

_____

- - - - - - - - - - - - - - - - -

_____

_____ sides

_____ vertices

_____ sides

_____ vertices

15. **TEXAS Test Prep** How many vertices does a triangle have?

○ 2   ○ 3   ○ 5

TAKE HOME ACTIVITY • Have your child draw a square, a trapezoid, and a triangle. For each shape, have him or her show you the sides and vertices, and tell how many of each.

Homework and Practice

TEKS Geometry and Measurement—1.6.B, 1.6.D
Also 1.6.A, 1.6.C
MATHEMATICAL PROCESSES 1.1.D, 1.1.E, 1.1.F, 1.1.G

Name _____

14.2 Attributes of Two-Dimensional Shapes

HANDS ON

Use to trace each straight side.
Use 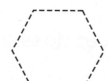 to circle each vertex (corner).
Write the number of sides and vertices (corners).

1. _____ sides

   _____ vertices

2. _____ sides

   _____ vertices

3. _____ sides

   _____ vertices

4. _____ sides

   _____ vertices

Problem Solving

Draw a picture to solve.

5. I am a shape with 6 straight sides and 6 vertices.

6. I am a shape with 4 straight sides that are not all the same length and 4 vertices.

Lesson Check

Choose the correct answer.

7. Max draws a shape with 3 straight sides and 3 vertices. Which shape does he draw?

   ○ rhombus   ○ triangle   ○ square

8. Leila draws a shape with 6 straight sides and 6 vertices. Which shape does she draw?

   ○ hexagon   ○ rhombus   ○ rectangle

9. How many vertices does a rhombus have?

   ○ 6   ○ 4   ○ 3

10. **Multi-step** Sofie has 13 shapes. There are triangles, rectangles, and hexagons. Four shapes have 3 straight sides. Two shapes are hexagons. How many shapes are rectangles?

    ○ 6   ○ 9   ○ 7

TEKS Geometry and Measurement—1.6.C, 1.6.F
MATHEMATICAL PROCESSES
1.1.E, 1.1.F

14.3
HANDS ON

Create Two-Dimensional Shapes

 Essential Question

How can you put two-dimensional shapes together to make new two-dimensional shapes?

Explore

Use pattern blocks. Draw to show your work.

 FOR THE TEACHER • Have children use pattern blocks to act out the following problem. Karen has some green pattern blocks. She made a shape with 3 sides and a shape with 4 sides. Draw the new shapes Karen could make.

Math Talk
Mathematical Processes

Describe the new shapes Karen made.

How many do you need to make a ⬡ ?

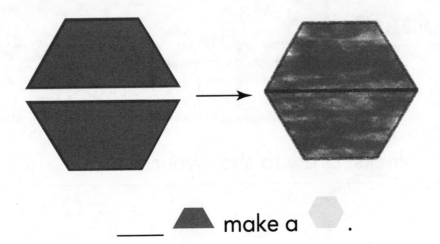

____ make a .

Use pattern blocks. Draw to show the blocks.
Write how many blocks you used.

1. How many ◆ make a ⬡ ? | ☑2. How many ▲ make a ▲ ?

____ ◆ make a ⬡ .   ____ ▲ make a .

Name _____

Problem Solving

Use pattern blocks. Draw to show the blocks.
Write how many blocks you used.

3. How many make a ?

⊘ 4. How many make a ?

____ make a .

____ make a .

5. **H.O.T.** Use me two times to make this shape. Which block am I? Circle a block to show your answer.

6. **H.O.T.** **Multi-Step** Use these pattern blocks to make the shape. Write how many times you used each block.

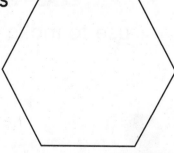

____ ____ ____

Use pattern blocks. Choose the correct answer.

7. Use some ▲ to make a larger triangle.
Draw the shape you made.
Then draw a triangle with a different shape.

8. **Multi-Step** Taylor used 3 ▨
to make a rectangle.
Draw the shape he made.

Then he used 4 ▨ to make
a square. Draw the shape
he made.

9. ⭐ **TEXAS Test Prep** How many ◆ do you
use to make a ⬡ ?

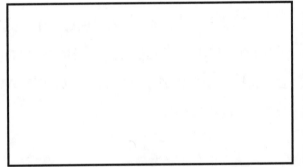

○ 6   ○ 3   ○ 2

TAKE HOME ACTIVITY • Have your child explain how he or she solved
Exercises 1 and 2.

14.3 HANDS ON — Create Two-Dimensional Shapes

Draw lines to show the shapes.

1. Draw lines to make this shape into 4 .

2. Draw a line to make this shape into 2 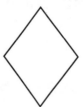.

 **Problem Solving** Real World

3. You could use me six times to make this shape. Which block am I? Circle a block to show your answer.

4. You could use me three times to make this shape. Which block am I? Circle a block to show your answer.

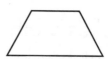

Choose the correct answer.

5. Jasmine makes this figure. Which shapes did she use?

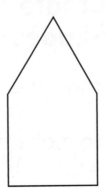

○ triangle and square

○ rhombus and rectangle

○ hexagon and rectangle

---

6. How many 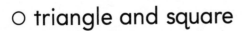 make a ▰ ?

○ 2   ○ 4   ○ 3

---

7. **Multi-Step** Caitlin makes this shape with blocks.

Tyler makes a different shape with the same number of blocks. Which shape does Tyler make?

○    ○    ○

TEKS Geometry and
Measurement—1.6.F

MATHEMATICAL PROCESSES
1.1.E, 1.1.F

14.4 Compose More Shapes

? Essential Question

How can you combine two-dimensional shapes to make new shapes?

Explore

Hands On

Use shapes to fill each outline.
Draw to show your work.

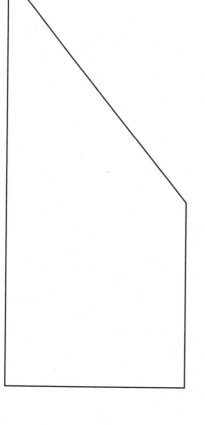

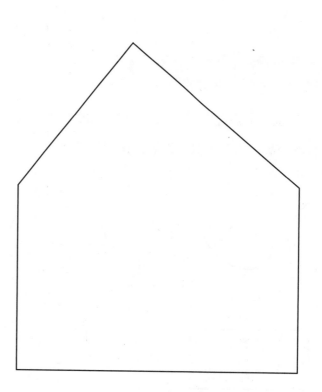

Math Talk

Mathematical Processes

Use the outline on the left to **describe** how two shapes can make another shape.

FOR THE TEACHER • Have children use two shapes to fill the outline on the left, and draw a line to show the two shapes. Then have children use three shapes to fill the outline on the right, again drawing lines to show the shapes.

Combine shapes to
make a new shape.

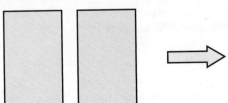 

or

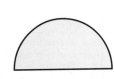 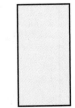

How else could you
combine 2 ?

Share and Show

Circle two shapes that can combine
to make the shape on the left.

1.

2.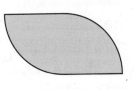

3.

Name _____

Problem Solving

Circle two shapes that can combine to make the shape on the left.

4.

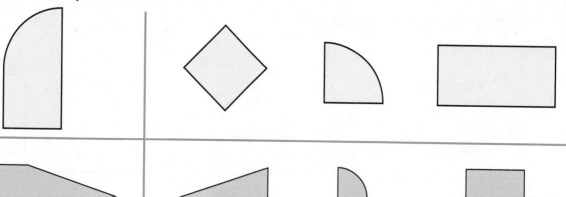

5.

H.O.T. **Multi-Step** Draw lines to show two different ways to combine the shapes on the left to make new shapes on the right.

Math on the Spot

6.

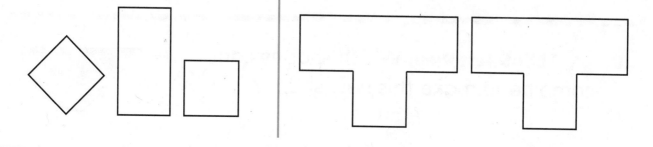

7.

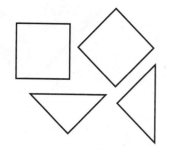

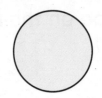
Choose the correct answer.

8. Analyze Which shapes can combine to make a circle?

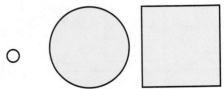

○   ○   ○

9. Multi-Step Alana builds this shape.

Esther takes the shape apart. She uses the same blocks. Which new shape could Esther build?

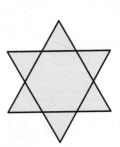

 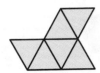   ○    ○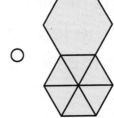

10. ⭐ **TEXAS Test Prep** Which shapes can combine to make this new shape?

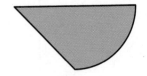

           ○   ○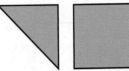

TAKE HOME ACTIVITY • Ask your child to draw a new shape he or she can make by combining two triangles.

14.4 Compose More Shapes

Circle two shapes that can combine to make the shape on the left.

1.

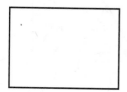  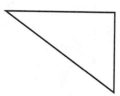

2.

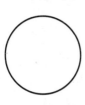

Problem Solving Real World

Multi-Step Draw lines to show two different ways to combine the shapes on the left to make new shapes on the right.

3.

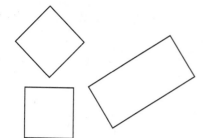

Choose the correct answer.

4. Which shapes can combine to
   make a square?

○ 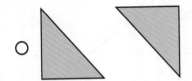   ○ 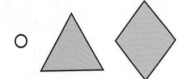   ○

5. Which shapes can combine to
   make this new shape?

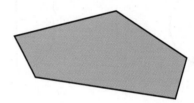

○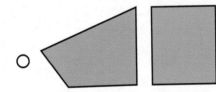

○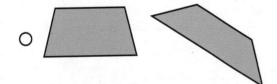

○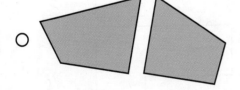

TEKS Geometry and Measurement—1.6.C, 1.6.F

MATHEMATICAL PROCESSES
1.1.B, 1.1.D, 1.1.E, 1.1.F

14.5 PROBLEM SOLVING • Create New Two-Dimensional Shapes

 Essential Question

How can acting it out help you make new shapes from combined shapes?

Unlock the Problem

Cora wants to combine shapes to make a circle.
She has ◺. How can Cora make a circle?

Read	Plan
What information am I given?	**What is my plan or strategy?**
Cora uses this shape.	I can _____ _____.

Solve

Show how to solve the problem.

Step 1 Use shapes. Combine to make a new shape.

 and   make⟩

Step 2 Then use the new shape.

 and   make⟩

 HOME CONNECTION • Recognizing how shapes can be put together and taken apart provides a foundation for future work with fractions.

Try Another Problem

Use shapes to solve.
Draw to show your work.

- What information am I given?
- What is my plan or strategy?

1. Use ☐ to make a larger ☐.

   Step 1 Combine shapes to make a new shape.

   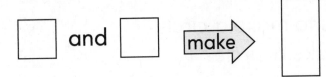

   Step 2 Then use the new shape.

   and [make ➡]

2. Use ◺ to make a ▭.

   Step 1 Combine shapes to make a new shape.

   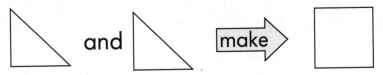

   Step 2 Then use the new shape.

   and [make ➡]

Math Talk
Mathematical Processes

Describe how you made the rectangle in Exercise 2.

Name _____

Use shapes to solve.
Draw to show your work.

☑**3.** Use 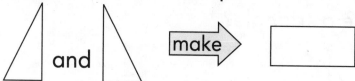 to make a ▢.

Step 1 Combine shapes to make a new shape.

△ and △ make ⟹ ▭

Step 2 Then use the new shape.

and **make** ⟹ ▢

Problem Solving

4. **H.O.T.** **Multi-Step** Use ⬭ and △
to make a ▱.

Step 1 Combine shapes to make a new shape.

⬭ and △  make ⟹ △

Step 2 Then use the new shape.

and

 make ⟹ ▱

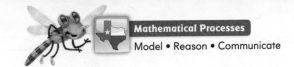
Daily Assessment Task

Choose the correct answer.

5. Reasoning Which two shapes make a circle?

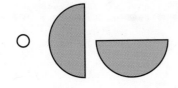 ○ 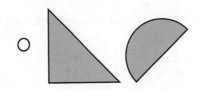 ○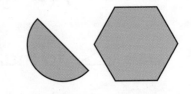

6. Which two shapes make a triangle?

○ 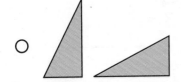   ○    ○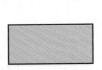

7. Multi-Step Gabe uses pattern blocks to make a new shape. He uses 1 and 3 . Which of these shapes can he make?

○ circle   ○ square   ○ hexagon

8. ⭐ **TEXAS Test Prep** Which new shape could you make?

○

Step 1
Combine ▢ and ◹ to make ◖.

Step 2
Then use ◖ and ◖.

○

○

 TAKE HOME ACTIVITY • Have your child explain how he or she solved Exercise 6.

14.5 PROBLEM SOLVING • Create New Two-Dimensional Shapes

Use shapes to solve. Draw to show your work.

1. Use ▱ to make a ⬡ .

Step 1 Combine shapes to make a new shape.

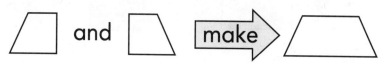

▱ and ▱ **make** ▱

Step 2 Then use the new shape.

and

make ⬡

Problem Solving Real World

2. **Multi-Step** Use △ and ◇ to make a ⬡ .

Step 1 Combine shapes to make a new shape.

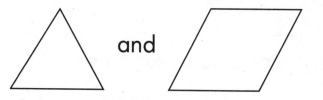 and **make**

Step 2 Then use the new shape.

and

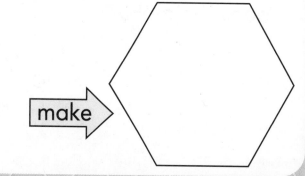

make

Choose the correct answer.

3. Which two shapes make a rectangle?

○ 　　○ 　　○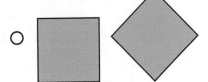

4. Nikki makes a star. She uses only 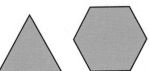 and ☐.
Which star does she make?

○ 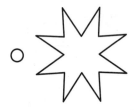　　○ 　　○

5. **Multi-Step** Jeanne uses pattern blocks to make a new

shape. She uses 4 ▲ and 1 ◆. Which new shape
does she make?

○ 　　○ 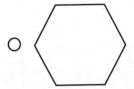　　○ ▭

Name _____

 ## Module 14 Assessment

Match each shape to its name. (pp. 514, 520)

1.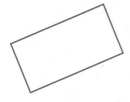

2.

3.

4.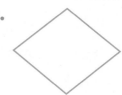

•   •   •   •

•   •   •   •

hexagon   triangle   rectangle   rhombus

Concepts and Skills

5. Circle the shapes that have only 3 vertices (corners). 🔹 1.6.A

Use pattern blocks. Draw to show the blocks.
Write how many blocks you use. 🔹 1.6.C, 1.6.F

6.

___ make a .

7.

___  make a .

8. How many straight sides
does a rhombus have? 1.6.D

○ 5   ○ 4   ○ 6

---

9. Which shapes can combine
to make this new shape? 1.6.F

○    ○    ○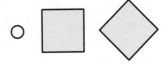

---

10. Which shapes can combine to
make this new shape? 1.6.F

○    ○    ○

---

11. Which new shape could
you make? 1.6C, 1.6.F

| Step 1 |
| Combine ⌐ and ⌐ to make ◗. |

| Step 2 |
| Then use ◗ and ◗. |

○   ○ ⬤   ○

TEKS Geometry and Measurement—1.6.E
MATHEMATICAL PROCESSES
1.1.C, 1.1.E, 1.1.F, 1.1.G

15.1
HANDS ON

Two-Dimensional Shapes on Three-Dimensional Solids

? Essential Question

What two-dimensional shapes do you see on the flat surfaces of three-dimensional solids?

 Explore Real World

 Hands On

Use a cone.

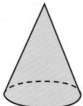

Math Talk
Mathematical Processes

What other solid could you use to draw the same kind of picture? **Explain.**

FOR THE TEACHER • Read the following problem, and have children use the workspace to act it out.
Lee places a cone on a piece of paper and draws around its flat surface. What does Lee draw?

Model and Draw

Trace around the **flat surfaces** of the three-dimensional solid to find the two-dimensional shapes.

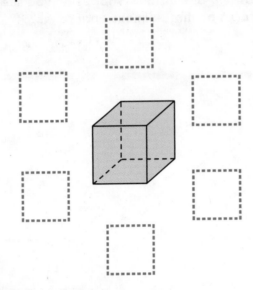

Share and Show

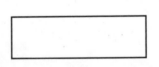

Use three-dimensional solids. Trace around the flat surfaces. Circle the shapes you draw.

1.

2.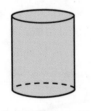

3.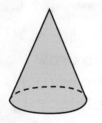

Problem Solving

Circle the objects you could trace to draw the shape.

4.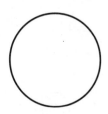

5.

6. **H.O.T.** Circle the solid that the pattern will make if you fold it and tape it together.

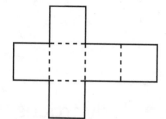 

7. **H.O.T.** **Multi-Step** Draw two different shapes you could make if you traced this solid.

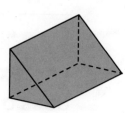

Choose the correct answer.

8. Carl buys a toy for his cat. The top and the bottom of the toy looks like this. Which shows the shape of the toy?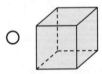

○   ○   ○

9. **Analyze** Donna buys a toy for her dog. Only the bottom of the toy looks like this. Which shows the shape of the toy?

○   ○   ○

10. **Multi-Step** Judy traces two sides of a solid. Draw the solid that she uses. Explain how you know that your answer is reasonable.

11. ⭐ **TEXAS Test Prep** Which flat surface does a cube have?

○   ○   ○

 TAKE HOME ACTIVITY • Collect a few three-dimensional objects that are shaped like spheres, cones, cylinders, and cubes. Ask your child what two-dimensional shapes are on those objects.

15.1
HANDS ON

Two-Dimensional Shapes on Three-Dimensional Solids

Look at the three-dimensional solid. Circle the shapes you would draw if you traced around the flat surfaces.

1.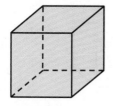

2.

Problem Solving

3. Draw a shape you could make if you traced this cube.

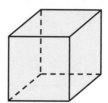

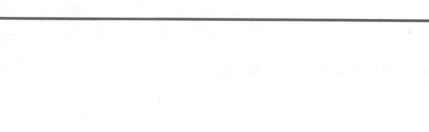

Choose the correct answer.

4. Maggie bakes a cake. The top and the bottom of the cake look like this. Which shows the shape of the cake?

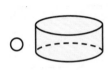 ○

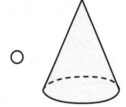 ○

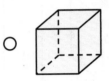 ○

5. **Multi-Step** Michael makes a board game in the shape of a rectangle. He traces around two faces of a solid. Which solid does he trace?

 ○

 ○

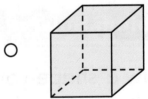 ○

6. Which flat surface does a cone have?

 ○

 ○

 ○

Name _____

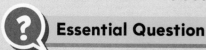

Attributes of Three-Dimensional Solids

? Essential Question
How can you identify and describe spheres, cones, and cylinders?

Explore

Draw to sort the three-dimensional solids.

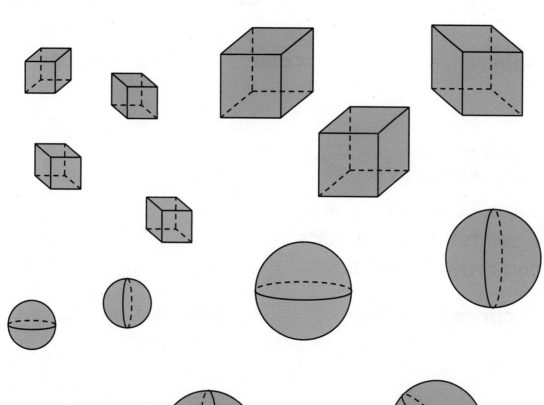

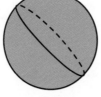

Math Talk
Mathematical Processes
Explain how you sorted the solids.

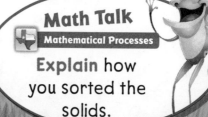

FOR THE TEACHER • Have children sort the three-dimensional solids into two groups. Have them draw around each group to show how they sorted.

Module 15

Look at the surfaces on these three-dimensional solids.
Some are flat. Some are curved.

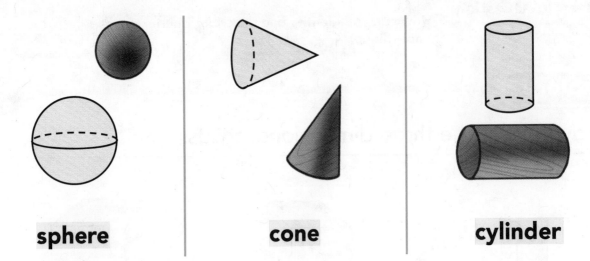

sphere   **cone**   **cylinder**

Share and Show   MATH BOARD

Use spheres, cones, and cylinders.
Sort the solids into two groups.
Name and draw the solids.

1. only a **curved surface**

 2. both flat and curved
   surfaces

Problem Solving

Use three-dimensional solids. Write the number of flat surfaces for each shape.

Exercises 3–5 can help you write the shape names.

3. A cylinder has _____ flat surfaces.

4. A cone has _____ flat surface.

5. A sphere has _____ flat surfaces.

H.O.T. Write to name each shape.

Math on the Spot

6.

sphere

7.

_ _ _ _ _ _ _ _ _ _ _ _

_ _ _ _ _ _ _ _ _ _ _ _

8.

_ _ _ _ _ _ _ _ _ _ _ _

_ _ _ _ _ _ _ _ _ _ _ _

9. **H.O.T.** **Multi-Step** Kelly drew objects that have both flat and curved surfaces. Circle the objects she drew.

Mathematical Processes
Model • Reason • Communicate

Choose the correct answer.

10. Lorna wins a toy that has no flat surfaces. Which solid is the shape of the toy she wins?

 ○   ○ 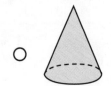   ○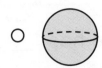

11. **Analyze** Gerri has a can that is shaped like a cylinder. How many flat surfaces does the can have?

○ 2   ○ 4   ○ 1

12. Which solid has only 1 flat surface?

○   ○ 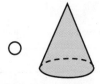   ○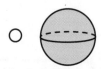

13. ⭐ **TEXAS Test Prep** Which solid has 2 flat surfaces?

○ 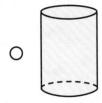   ○    ○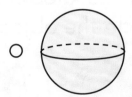

 TAKE HOME ACTIVITY • Ask your child to name real objects shaped like a sphere, a cone, and a cylinder.

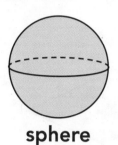
Name _____

15.2
HANDS ON

Attributes of Three-Dimensional Solids

sphere

cylinder

cone

Draw each solid.

1.	2.	3.
cone	cylinder	sphere

Problem Solving

Write the name of each solid shape.

4. A _____ has 0 flat surfaces.

5. A _____ has 1 flat surface.

6. A _____ has 2 flat surfaces.

Choose the correct answer.

7. Emma plays a music toy with a curved surface and 2 flat surfaces. Which solid is the shape of the toy she plays?

○ 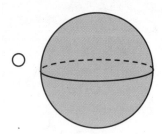   ○ 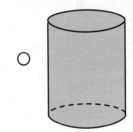   ○

8. Jason has a toy shaped like a sphere. How many flat surfaces does the toy have?

○ 0   ○ 1   ○ 2

9. Bailey used blocks to build a tower. She used blocks with 2 flat surfaces. Which block did she use?

○ 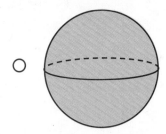   ○ 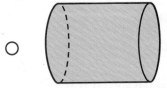   ○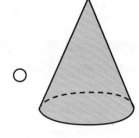

10. **Multi-Step** Which solid has a flat surface and a curved surface?

○ 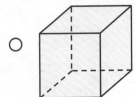   ○    ○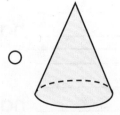

Name _____

15.3
HANDS ON

More Three-Dimensional Solids

? Essential Question

How can you identify and describe rectangular prisms, cubes, and triangular prisms?

Explore

Hands On

Draw to sort the three-dimensional solids.

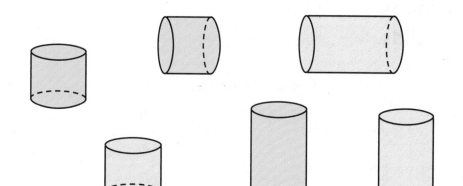

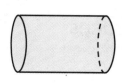

Math Talk
Mathematical Processes

Explain how you sorted the solids.

FOR THE TEACHER • Have children sort the three-dimensional solids into two groups. Have them draw around each group to show how they sorted.

Module 15

Model and Draw

Look at the faces, the vertices, and the edges of these solids.

Why is cube a special kind of rectangular prism?

THINK
A face is a flat surface of a solid.
An edge is where 2 faces meet.
A vertex is where 3 or more edges meet.

rectangular prism

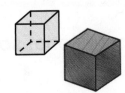

cube

triangular prism

Share and Show

Use rectangular prisms, cubes, and triangular prisms.
Sort the solids into groups.
Name and draw the solids.

1. 6 faces

✓2. 5 faces

3. 9 edges

✓4. 8 vertices

Problem Solving

Use three-dimensional solids. Write how many.

Solid	Number of Faces	Number of Edges	Number of Vertices
5.	_____ faces	_____ edges	_____ vertices
6.	_____ faces	_____ edges	_____ vertices
7.	_____ faces	_____ edges	_____ vertices

8. **H.O.T.** How many faces of a cube are squares?

_____ faces

9. **H.O.T.** **Multi-Step** Which solid has some faces that are triangles and some faces that are rectangles? **Explain.**

_____

_____

_____

_____

Choose the correct answer.

10. **Representations** Terri uses this block to build a house. What is the solid?

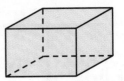

○ cube ○ rectangular prism ○ cylinder

11. Johnny builds a birdhouse. It has 6 faces. The faces are all squares that are the same size. Which shows the shape of Johnny's birdhouse?

○ 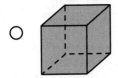 ○ 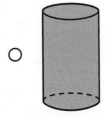 ○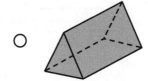

12. **Multi-Step** Louis builds an object with only triangles and rectangles. Which object does he build?

○   ○ 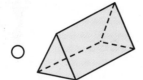 ○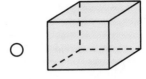

13. ⭐ **TEXAS Test Prep** Which solid has 5 faces?

○ 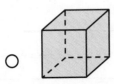 ○ 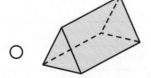 ○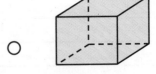

 HOME CONNECTION • Ask your child to name real objects shaped like a rectangular prism, a cube, and a triangular prism.

TEKS Geometry and Measurement—1.6.B, 1.6.E
MATHEMATICAL PROCESSES 1.1.D, 1.1.E, 1.1.F, 1.1.G

Name _____

15.3 More Three-Dimensional Solids

HANDS ON

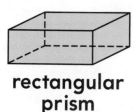

rectangular prism

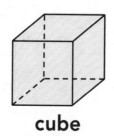

cube

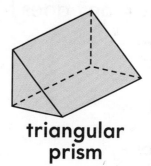

triangular prism

Name and draw a solid to match.

1. 5 faces

2. 8 vertices

Problem Solving

3. How many faces of a cube are squares? _____ faces

4. How many faces of a triangular prism are rectangles? _____ faces

5. How many faces of a triangular prism are triangles? _____ faces

Choose the correct answer.

6. Sam finds a small cube. He counts the vertices. How many does he count?

   o 5

   o 6

   o 8

7. Jackie chooses a triangular prism. She counts the edges. How many edges does she count?

   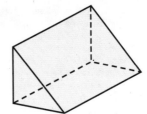

   o 9

   o 12

   o 6

8. **Multi-Step** How many more vertices does a cube have than a triangular prism?

   o 1

   o 2

   o 8

9. Which solid has 9 edges?

   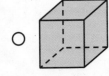 o   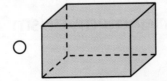 o   o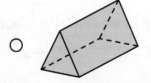

Name _____

15.4 PROBLEM SOLVING • Three-Dimensional Solids

? Essential Question

How can making a model help you identify and describe three-dimensional solids?

Unlock the Problem

Emma wants to draw an object for this riddle.

> I am a toy.
> I have only a curved surface.

Read	Plan
What information am I given?	**What is my plan or strategy?**
The object is a __toy__ with only a _____ surface.	I can _____ _____.

Solve

Show how you solve the problem.
I look at the solids that have a curved surface.

A sphere has only a curved surface.
A ball is a toy that is a sphere.

 HOME CONNECTION • Your child solved this problem by looking at models of three-dimensional solids and finding a model with only a curved surface.

Module 15

five hundred sixty-three **563**

Draw an object for the riddle. Use models of solids to help you.

- What information am I given?
- What is my plan or strategy?

1.

I am a block.
I have 6 faces that are squares.
Draw me.

2.

I am a hat.
I have 1 flat surface.
I have 1 curved surface.
Draw me.

3.

I am a box.
I have 2 faces that are squares.
I have 4 faces that are rectangles.
Draw me.

Math Talk
Mathematical Processes

How does making a model help you solve a riddle?

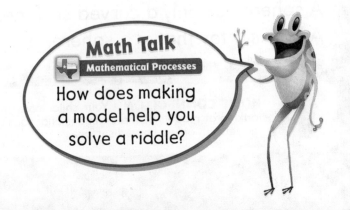

Name _____

Draw an object for the riddle. Use models of solids to help you.

✓ 4.

> I am a can.
> I have 2 flat surfaces.
> I have I curved surface.
> Draw me.

Problem Solving

5.

> I am a box.
> I have 2 faces that are triangles.
> I have 3 faces that are rectangles.
> Draw me.

6. **H.O.T.** Multi-Step

> I am a block.
> I have 6 faces.
> I have 8 vertices.
> Draw two different blocks I could be.

Daily Assessment Task

Choose the correct answer.

7. Analyze Tim has a toy that is shaped like a sphere. Which toy does Tim have?

8. Mari picks a block with flat and curved surfaces. Which block does she pick?

9. Multi-Step David puts two blocks together to make a rectangular prism. Which blocks does David use?

  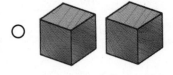

10. ⭐ **TEXAS Test Prep** Which solid is a triangular prism?

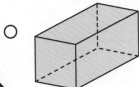 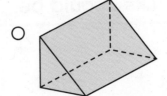 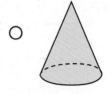

 HOME CONNECTION • Have your child explain how he or she solved one of the problems in this lesson.

15.4 PROBLEM SOLVING • Three-Dimensional Solids

Draw an object for the riddle.

1.
> I have a curved surface.
> I have no flat surfaces.
> Draw me.

2.
> I am a block.
> I have I flat surface.
> I have I curved surface.
> Draw me.

Problem Solving

3.
> I am a block.
> I have 3 faces that are rectangles.
> I have 2 faces that are triangles.
> Draw me.

Choose the correct answer.

4. Wendy finds a toy that is shaped like a cube. Which toy does Wendy find?

○    ○    ○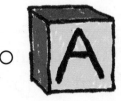

5. **Multi-Step** Winston puts four blocks together to make a tall cylinder. Which blocks does Winston use?

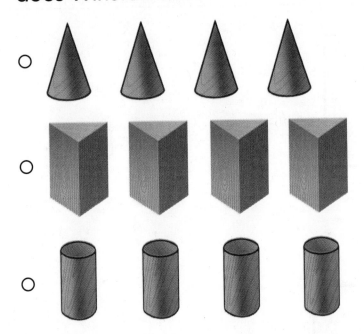

6. Which solid is a rectangular prism?

○ 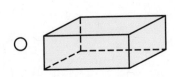   ○ 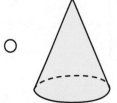   ○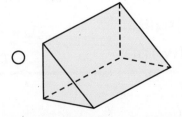

Module 15 Assessment

Vocabulary

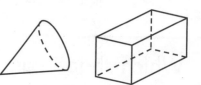

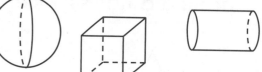

1. Color the **cube** with . (p. 558)

2. Color the **cone** with . (p. 552)

3. Color the **cylinder** with  . (p. 552)

Concepts and Skills

4. Circle the objects you could trace to draw the shape. ☛ TEKS 1.6.E

5. Circle the object below that has only a curved surface. ☛ TEKS 1.6.E

6. Draw a line under the objects below that have both curved and flat surfaces. ☛ TEKS 1.6.E

7. Which number completes the sentence?
A rectangular prism has ___?___ faces. ⬇ TEKS 1.6.E

○ 8   ○ 6   ○ 4

---

8. Which shape can you draw if you trace
around a flat surface of a cube? ⬇ TEKS 1.6.E

○   ○   ○

---

9. Which solid has 6 faces? ⬇ TEKS 1.6.E

                      ○

---

10. Which solid has 6 vertices? ⬇ TEKS 1.6.E

 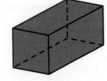   ○   ○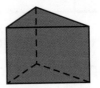

---

11. Which solid matches the
riddle? ⬇ TEKS 1.6.E

I am a block.
I have 8 vertices.
I have 12 edges.

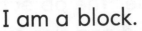

○   ○ 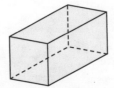   ○

Name _____

16.1 Equal or Unequal Parts

? Essential Question

How can you identify equal and unequal parts in two-dimensional shapes?

Explore Real World   Hands On

Draw to show the parts.

Show 2 .

Show 3 △.

Math Talk
Mathematical Processes

Are all of the triangles the same? **Explain.**

FOR THE TEACHER • Have children draw lines to show two triangles in one square and three triangles in the other square.

Model and Draw

These show **equal parts**, or **equal shares**.

These show **unequal parts**, or **unequal shares**.

How can you describe equal shares?

Share and Show

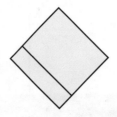
MATH BOARD

Describe the parts.
Write **equal parts** or **unequal parts**.

THINK
Are the parts the same size?

1.

_____

2.

_____

✓3.

_____

4.

_____

5.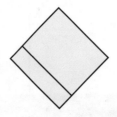

_____

✓6.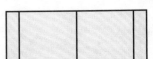

_____

Name _____

Color the shapes that show unequal shares.

7.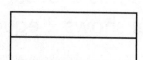

Color the shapes that show equal shares.

8.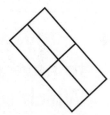

H.O.T. Write the number of equal shares.

9.

_____ equal shares

10.

_____ equal shares

H.O.T. **Multi-Step** Draw lines to show the parts.

11. 2 equal shares

2 unequal shares

12. 4 equal shares

4 unequal shares

Choose the correct answer.

13. Gordon has a wheel of cheese.
He will share this cheese with Denny.
Which wheel shows 2 equal parts?

 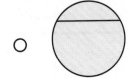 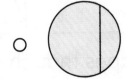

14. Analyze Lena is cutting a square cake
to have equal shares with 3 friends.
Which square shows 4 equal parts?

 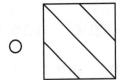

15. Multi-Step Henry has a loaf of bread
shaped like a rectangle. He wants to cut it
into two equal parts. Then he wants to cut
each part into two more equal parts. How
many parts will Henry have?

○ 2   ○ 6   ○ 4

16. ⭐ **TEXAS Test Prep** Which shows equal shares?

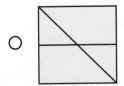 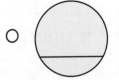

 TAKE HOME ACTIVITY • Draw a circle on a piece of paper. Ask your
child to draw a line so the circle shows 2 equal shares.

TEKS Geometry and Measurement—1.6.G, 1.6.H
MATHEMATICAL PROCESSES 1.1.D, 1.1.E, 1.1.F, 1.1.G

Name _____

16.1 Equal or Unequal Parts

Circle the shape that shows unequal parts.

1.

2.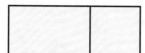

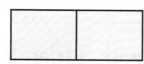

3.

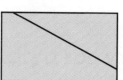

Color the shapes that show equal parts.

4.

Problem Solving

Write **equal** or **unequal** to describe the parts.

5. 4 _____
shares

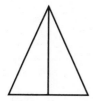

6. 4 _____
shares

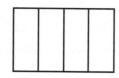

7. 2 _____
shares

Choose the correct answer.

8. Ginger has a cheese sandwich. She will share the sandwich with her sister. Which sandwich shows 2 equal parts?

○ 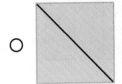   ○    ○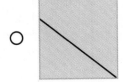

9. Lucy has a pizza to share with 3 friends. She wants everyone to get an equal share. Which pizza shows 4 equal parts?

○ 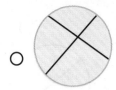   ○    ○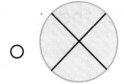

10. **Multi-Step** Hank has a ball of dough. He wants to cut it into 2 equal parts. Then he wants to cut each part into 2 more equal parts. How many parts will Hank have?

○ 2   ○ 4   ○ 8

11. Which shows equal shares?

○    ○ 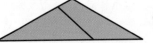   ○

TEKS Geometry and
Measurement—1.6.G,
1.6.H
MATHEMATICAL PROCESSES
1.1.D, 1.1.E, 1.1.F, 1.1.G

16.2 Halves

 Essential Question

How can a shape be separated into two equal shares?

Explore Real World Hands On

Draw to solve.

 FOR THE TEACHER • Have children draw
to solve this problem: Two friends share the
sandwich on the left. How can they cut the
sandwich so each gets an equal share? Then have
children solve this problem: Two other friends
share the sandwich on the right. How could this sandwich
be cut a different way so each friend gets an equal share?

Math Talk
Mathematical Processes

Will all four friends
get the same amount
of sandwich?
Explain.

The 2 equal shares make 1 whole.

2 equal shares

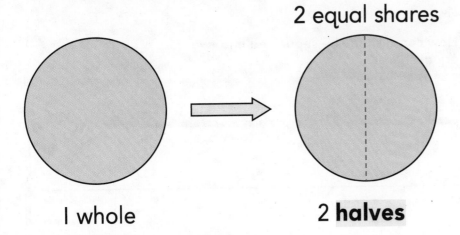

1 whole

2 **halves**

Is **half of** the circle larger or smaller than the whole circle?

Share and Show

MATH BOARD

Draw a line to show halves.

1.

☑2.

3.

☑4.

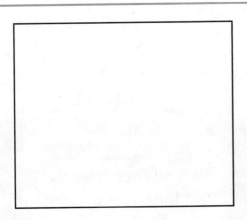

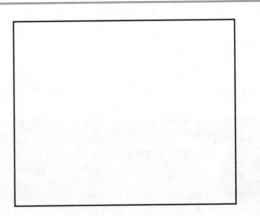

Problem Solving

Name the parts.
Write **halves** or **not halves**.

5.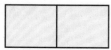

_____

6.

_____

7.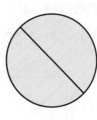

_____

8.

_____

9.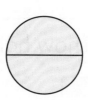

_____

10.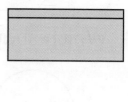

_____

11. **H.O.T.** Use the picture.
Write numbers to solve.

The picture shows _____ halves.

The _____ equal shares make _____ whole.

12. **H.O.T.** **Multi-Step** Draw three different
ways to show halves.

Mathematical Processes
Model • Reason • Communicate

Choose the correct answer.

13. Sandy has a whole sandwich. She shares an equal part with her friend. Which shows halves?

○ 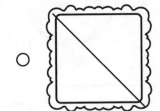   ○    ○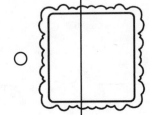

14. Which shape does **not** show halves?

○ 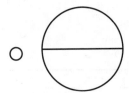   ○   ○

15. **Reasoning** Use 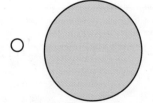 to help you.
Kevin has three halves of a circle.
How many whole circles does Kevin have?

○ 1   ○ 3   ○ 2

16. ⭐ **TEXAS Test Prep** Which shows halves?

○ 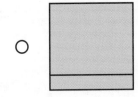   ○   ○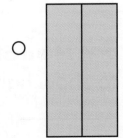

 TAKE HOME ACTIVITY • Draw a rectangle on a piece of paper. Ask your child to draw a line to show halves.

Name _____

16.2 Halves

Draw a line to show halves.

1.
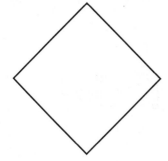

2.
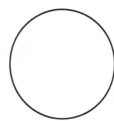

3.
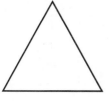

4.
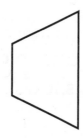

Problem Solving

Multi-Step Draw three different ways to show halves.

5.
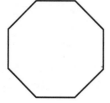 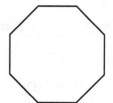

6.

Choose the correct answer.

7. Becca has a dog cookie for her dogs Daisy and Champ. Which shows halves?

○    ○    ○

8. Jose cuts paper hearts into two equal parts. Which shows halves?

○    ○    ○

9. Use ⌓ to help you.
Nia has five halves of a circle. How many whole circles does Nia have?

○ 2

○ 1

○ 3

TEKS Geometry and Measurement—1.6.G, 1.6.H
MATHEMATICAL PROCESSES
1.1.D, 1.1.E, 1.1.F, 1.1.G

16.3 Fourths

? Essential Question

How can a shape be separated into four equal shares?

Explore

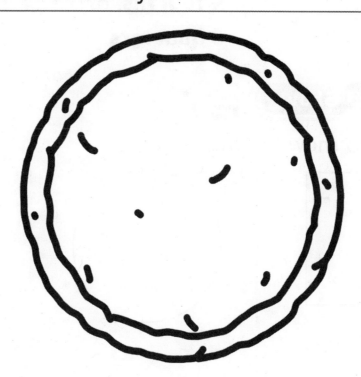

Use what you know about halves.
Draw to solve. Write how many.

There are _____ equal shares.

Math Talk
Mathematical Processes
How did you decide how to cut the pizza? Explain.

FOR THE TEACHER • Read the following problem. Two friends will share a pizza. Then two more friends come. Now four friends will share the pizza. How can the pizza be cut so each friend gets an equal share? How many equal shares are there?

Model and Draw

The 4 equal shares make 1 whole.

4 equal shares

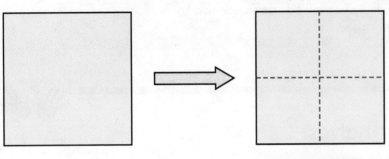

1 whole

4 **fourths**, or
4 **quarters**

How can you
describe one of the
4 equal shares?

Share and Show

Draw lines to show fourths.

1.

2.
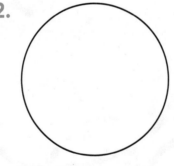

3.

4.
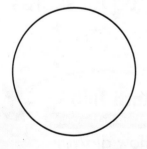

5.
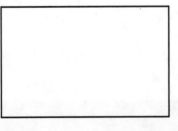

6.
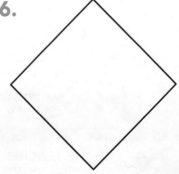

Name _____

Name the parts.
Write **fourths** or **not fourths**.

7.

_____

8.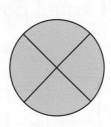

_____

9.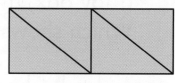

_____

10.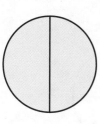

_____

11.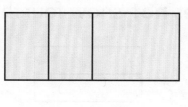

_____

12.

_____

13. **H.O.T.** Circle the shape that
shows quarters.

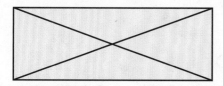 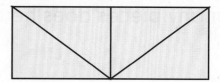

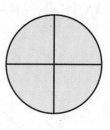

14. **H.O.T.** **Multi-Step** Draw three different
ways to show fourths.

 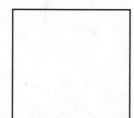 

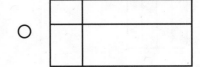

Mathematical Processes
Model • Reason • Communicate

Choose the correct answer.

15. Representations Mick wants to build a toy box. It will have 4 equal parts. Which shows fourths?

16. Which shape does **not** show fourths.

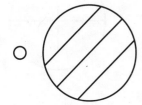 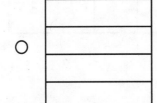 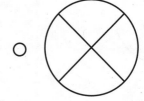

17. Multi-Step Billy will share his cake with 3 friends. Each person will get a fourth. He hands out 1 piece. He eats 1 piece. How many pieces does he have left?

○ 2   ○ 4   ○ 1

18. ⭐ **TEXAS Test Prep** Which shows fourths?

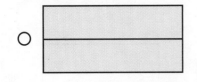 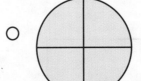 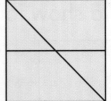

TAKE HOME ACTIVITY • Draw a circle on a piece of paper. Ask your child to draw lines to show fourths.

16.3 Fourths

Color a fourth of the shape.

1.

2.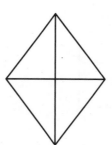

3.

Color a quarter of the shape.

4.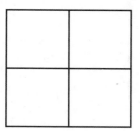

5.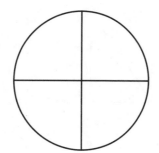

6.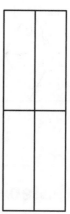

Problem Solving

Draw three different ways to show fourths.

7.

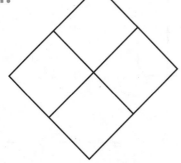

Choose the correct answer.

8. Tina wants to paint a wall. The wall will have 4 equal parts. Which shows fourths?

 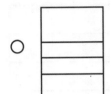   ○ 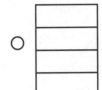   ○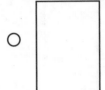

9. Which shows quarters?

○ 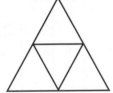   ○    ○

10. **Multi-Step** Isabelle shares a pizza with her mother, her brother, and her father. Each person will get a fourth. She hands out 2 pieces. She eats 1 piece. How many pieces does she have left?

○ 0

○ 3

○ 1

Name _____

 Module 16 Assessment

Draw a line to show **halves.** (p. 578)

1. 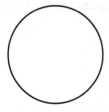   2.    3.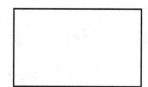

Draw lines to show **fourths.** (p. 584)

4. 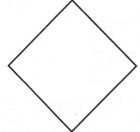   5. 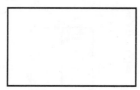   6.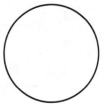

Concepts and Skills

7. Color the shapes that show unequal shares. ↓ TEKS 1.6.G, 1.6.H

---

8. Color the shapes that show equal shares. ↓ TEKS 1.6.G, 1.6.H

      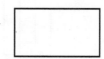

9. Which shows halves? TEKS 1.6.G, 1.6.H

○ 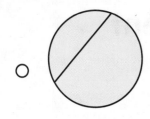   ○ 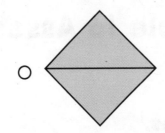   ○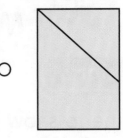

10. Which shape shows unequal parts? TEKS 1.6.G, 1.6.H

○ 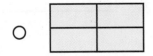   ○ 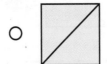   ○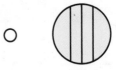

11. Which shading shows half of a square? TEKS 1.6.G, 1.6.H

○    ○ 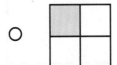   ○

12. Which shape shows fourths? TEKS 1.6.G, 1.6.H

○ 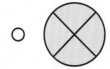   ○    ○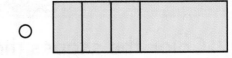

13. Which shading shows a quarter of a rectangle? TEKS 1.6.G, 1.6.H

○ 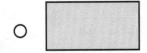   ○ 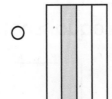   ○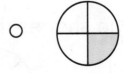

TEKS Geometry and Measurement—1.7.A

MATHEMATICAL PROCESSES 1.1.C

17.1 Length
HANDS ON

? Essential Question How do you use measuring tools to measure length?

Explore Real World

Hands On

Use objects to show the problem.
Draw to show your work.

FOR THE TEACHER • Read the problem. Have children use classroom objects to act it out. Rosa has something that is longer than the drinking straw. She has another object that is shorter than the key. What objects might she have?

Math Talk
Mathematical Processes
Compare the straw and the key. Which is longer? Which is shorter? Explain.

You can use string to measure the **length** of the pencil box.

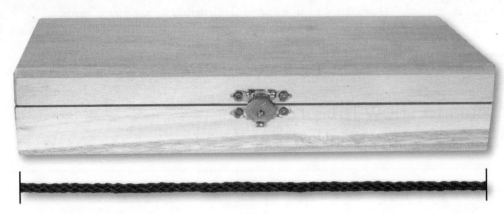

The string is as long as the pencil box.

Share and Show

Objects longer than the string will **not** fit.

Use the string as a tool to measure the objects.
Circle the objects that will fit in the pencil box.

1.

2.

✓3.

✓4.

Name _____

Use the string as a tool to measure the objects. Circle the objects that will fit in the pencil box.

REMEMBER
The string is as long as the pencil box.

5.

6.

Solve.

7. **H.O.T.** **Multi-Step** Barry is sending Jake his skateboard in a box. He used a ribbon to measure the skateboard. Explain how long the box needs to be?

8. **H.O.T.** A box is as long as this ribbon. Find and draw an object that will fit in the box.

Explain how you know the object will fit inside.

_____

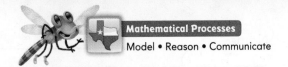
Choose the correct answer.

9. **Multi-Step** A box is the same length as the ribbon. The ribbon is longer than the pencil. The ribbon is shorter than the straw and the spoon. Which object will fit in the box?

○ straw   ○ pencil   ○ spoon

Explain why the other objects are not good choices.

_____

10. ⭐ **TEXAS Test Prep** A box is the same length as this string. Use string to find which object will fit in the box.

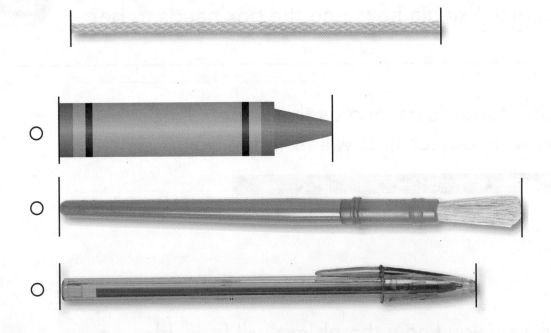

TAKE HOME ACTIVITY • Have your child explain to you how he or she uses a measuring tool to measure an object.

17.1 Length
HANDS ON

Use string this long as a tool to measure the objects.

Circle the objects that are longer than the string.

1.

2.

3.

Problem Solving Real World

4. Ava wants to make a bracelet as long as this piece of yarn. Draw a bracelet as long as the yarn.

Explain how you know the bracelet and yarn are the same length.

_____

- -

_____

Choose the correct answer.

5. A pencil case is the same length as this string. Use string to find which pencil will fit in the box.

○

○

○

6. Elena wants to put objects inside this box.

Which length of ribbon will be the best measuring tool to measure the length of the objects?

○

○

○

Name _____

TEKS Geometry and Measurement—1.7.B, 1.7.D
Also 1.7.A
MATHEMATICAL PROCESSES
1.1.C, 1.1.E

17.2 HANDS ON
Use Nonstandard Units to Measure Length

 Essential Question

How do you measure length using nonstandard units?

Draw to show the problem.

Math Talk
Mathematical Processes

How do you draw the boat to be the right length? **Explain.**

FOR THE TEACHER • Read the problem. Jimmy sees that his boat is about 6 color tiles long. Draw Jimmy's boat. Draw the color tiles to show how you measured.

Module 17

five hundred ninety-seven **597**

Model and Draw

You can use to measure length.
Write how many.

Each  is a **unit**

about _____

Share and Show

Use real objects. Use to measure.

1.

about _____

2.

about _____

☑ **3.**

about _____

☑ **4.**

about _____

Problem Solving

Use real objects. Use 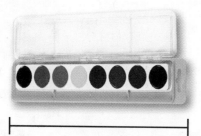 to measure.

5.

about _____ ⬛

6.

about _____ ⬛

---

7. **H.O.T.** The green yarn is about 2 ⬛ long. About how long is the blue yarn?

about _____ ⬛

---

8. **H.O.T.** **Multi-Step** Use ⬛. Bo has 4 ribbons. Circle the ribbon that is less than 3 ⬛ long but more than 1 ⬛ long.

Daily Assessment Task

Use real objects. Choose the correct answer.

9. **Representations** About how many 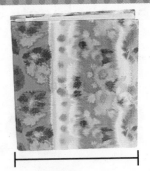 long is a book?

○ about 5 ■ | ○ about 14 ■ | ○ about 1 ■

10. About how many ■ long is a shoe?

○ about 2 ■ | ○ about 4 ■ | ○ about 6 ■

11. The craft stick is about 4 ■ long.
About how long is the spoon?

○ about 3 ■
○ about 8 ■
○ about 5 ■

12. ⭐ **TEXAS Test Prep** Use ■. Ray measures the key with ■. About how long is the key?

○ about 2 ■
○ about 1 ■
○ about 3 ■

TAKE HOME ACTIVITY • Give your child paper clips or other small objects that are the same length. Have him or her use the paper clips to measure objects around the house.

© Houghton Mifflin Harcourt Publishing Company • Image Credits: (spoon) ©Stockbyte/Getty Images; (key) ©Chloe Johnson/Alamy

17.2
HANDS ON

Use Nonstandard Units to Measure Length

Use real objects. Use  to measure.

1.

about _____

2.

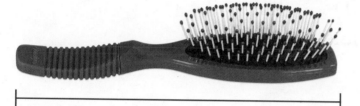

about _____

3.

about _____

Problem Solving

4. Multi-Step The top worm is about
1  long. About how long is the
bottom worm?

about _____

Choose the correct answer.

5. About how many  long is a scraper?

  ○ about 2 ⊂⊃

  ○ about 13 ⊂⊃

  ○ about 5 ⊂⊃

6. The pencil is about 10 ⊂⊃ long.
   About how long is the stapler?

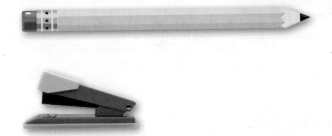

  ○ about 4 ⊂⊃

  ○ about 10 ⊂⊃

  ○ about 1 ⊂⊃

7. Alia measures the chalk with ⊂⊃.
   About how long is the chalk?

  ○ about 1 ⊂⊃

  ○ about 20 ⊂⊃

  ○ about 3 ⊂⊃

TEKS Geometry and Measurement—1.7.B, 1.7.D

Also 1.7.A

MATHEMATICAL PROCESSES
1.1.C, 1.1.E

17.3
HANDS ON

Make a Nonstandard Measuring Tool

? **Essential Question**

How do you use a nonstandard measuring tool to measure length?

Explore Real World

Hands On

Circle the name of the child who measured correctly.

Alli

Sid

 FOR THE TEACHER • Read the problem. Sid and Alli measure the same pencil. Sid says it is about 4 paper clips long. Alli says it is about 3 paper clips long. Circle the name of the child who measured correctly.

Math Talk
Mathematical Processes

Explain how you know who measured correctly.

Model and Draw

Make your own paper clip measuring tool like the one on the shelf. Measure the length of a door. About how long is the door?

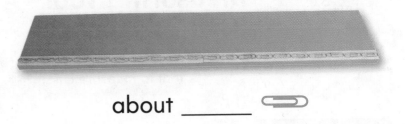

about _____

Share and Show

Use real objects and the measuring tool you made to measure.

1.

about _____

2.

about _____

✓3.

about _____

✓4.

about _____

Name _____

Use the measuring tool you made.
Measure real objects.

5.  about _____

6. about _____

Solve.

7. **H.O.T.** Lisa tried to measure the pencil.
She thinks the pencil is 5 paper clips long.
About how long is the pencil?

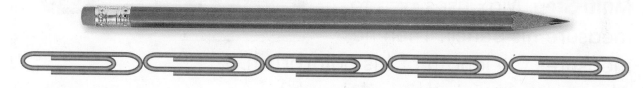

about _____

8. **H.O.T.** **Multi-Step** Cody
measured his real lunch box.
It is about 10  long.
About how long is Cody's
real pencil?

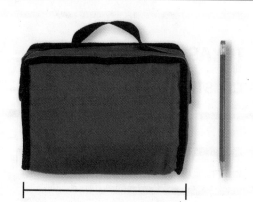

Cody's lunch box
and pencil

about _____

Mathematical Processes
Model • Reason • Communicate

Choose the correct answer.

9. **Representations** Evan uses  to measure his paddle. About how many ▬▬▬ long is the paddle?

○ about 4 ▬▬ | ○ about 6 ▬▬ | ○ about 5 ▬▬

10. Sophie uses ⬭ to measure her necklace. About how long is the necklace?

○ about 9 ⬭ | ○ about 10 ⬭ | ○ about 8 ⬭

11. **Multi-Step** Max uses ⬭ to measure his pencil. Then he measures the length of his paintbrush. About how long is the paintbrush?

○ about 3 ⬭ | ○ about 8 ⬭ | ○ about 5 ⬭

12. ⭐**TEXAS Test Prep** Use ⬭.
Which string is about 3 ⬭ long?

○ ━━━━━━━━━━━━

○ ━━━━━━━━

○ ━━━━━

TAKE HOME ACTIVITY • Have your child measure different objects around the house using a paper clip measuring tool.

606 six hundred six

17.3
HANDS ON

Make a Nonstandard Measuring Tool

Use a paper clip measuring tool. Measure real objects.

I.

about _____

2.

about _____

3.

about _____

4.

about _____

Choose the correct answer.

5. Keisha uses ▭▶ to measure her stuffed bear. About how many ▭▶ long is the bear?

○ about 2 ▭▶

○ about 8 ▭▶

○ about 1 ▭▶

---

6. **Multi-Step** Chase uses ▭▶ to measure his toy truck. Then he measures his toy car. About how long is the toy car?

○ about 1 ▭▶   ○ about 2 ▭▶   ○ about 6 ▭▶

---

7. Use ⬭. Which string is about 2 ⬭ long?

○ ⬤━━━━━━━━━━

○ ⬤━━━━━━━

○ ⬤━━━

Name _____

17.4 PROBLEM SOLVING • Explore Length

? Essential Question

How can acting it out help you solve a problem about nonstandard units to measure length?

🔑 Unlock the Problem 🌎

April measures the length of her book with 2 different units. She uses and _____.
Which measurement uses the greater number of units?

Each and _____ is a unit .

Read	Plan
What information am I given?	**What is my plan or strategy?**
Measure the book using and _____.	I can _____ _____.

Solve

Show how you solve the problem.

_____   _____ _____

Solve. Draw or write to explain.

1. Choose two different measuring tools to measure the distance from your desk to the wall. Draw the units, and write how many of each unit you used to measure. How are the measurements different?

_____

_ _

_____

_____

_ _

_____

2. Choose two different measuring tools to measure a folder. Draw a picture to show each measurement, and explain why they are different.

_____

_ _

_____

_____

_ _

_____

Math Talk
Mathematical Processes

Why does it take fewer of a unit to measure an object? Explain.

Name _____

Solve. Draw or write to explain.

3. The bookmark is about 2  long. Mark measures the same bookmark and finds it is 8 ▪ long. Explain why Mark's measurement uses more units.

_____

- - - - - - - - - - - - - - - - - - - -

_____

- - - - - - - - - - - - - - - - - - - -

_____

- - - - - - - - - - - - - - - - - - - -

_____

Problem Solving

4. **H.O.T.** **Multi-Step** Erica chose ⊂⊃ to measure an eraser. Allan chose ▭ to measure the same eraser. Which unit would you choose? Explain.

_____

- - - - - - - - - - - - - - - - - - - -

_____

- - - - - - - - - - - - - - - - - - - -

_____

- - - - - - - - - - - - - - - - - - - -

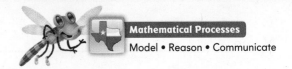
Daily Assessment Task

Use real objects. Choose the correct answer.

5. **Justify** Grace measures the table with ▪ and ∼∼∼∼∼. She uses more ▪ than ∼∼∼∼∼. Which describes why she uses more ▪

   ○ the ▪ is the same length as the ∼∼∼∼∼

   ○ the ▪ is shorter than the ∼∼∼∼∼

   ○ the ▪ is longer than the ∼∼∼∼∼

6. Roger measures his baseball bat using a ▭▭▭▭ and a ▬▬▬▬.
   He uses more ▭▭▭▭.
   Which describes how the measurements are different?

   ○ the ▭▭▭▭ is shorter so he needs more ▭▭▭▭ than ▬▬▬▬

   ○ the ▭▭▭▭ is the same length so he needs the same number of ▬▬▬▬

   ○ the ▭▭▭▭ is longer so he needs fewer ▭▭▭▭ than ▬▬▬▬

7. ⭐ **TEXAS Test Prep** Which shows the correct way to measure a desk using two units of different length?

   ○ [paper clips and pencils]

   ○ [paper clips and pencils]

   ○ [paper clip and pencil]

TAKE HOME ACTIVITY • Have your child measure an object with paper clips and then with craft sticks. Ask him or her why more paper clips were used to measure the object.

6I2 six hundred twelve

Homework and Practice

Name _____

17.4 PROBLEM SOLVING • Explore Length

Draw or write to explain.

1. Ella measures a book. It is about 9 ▭ long. Sam measures the same book and finds it is 3 ▭ long. Explain why Sam's measurement is fewer units.

_____

_____

_____

_____

Problem Solving

2. Nate chose a ▭ to measure the length of a crayon. Mara chose ▭ to measure the length of a crayon. Which unit would you choose? Explain.

_____

_____

_____

_____

Choose the correct answer.

3. Faith measures the beach towel with ▬ and ⊂⊃. She uses fewer ▬ than ⊂⊃. Which describes why she uses fewer ▬?

○ the ▬ and the ⊂⊃ are the same length.

○ the ▬ is longer than the ⊂⊃.

○ the ⊂⊃ is longer than the ▬.

4. Danielle measures her dog leash using a ▪ and a ▬. She uses fewer ▬. Which describes how the measurements are different?

○ the ▬ is longer so she needs fewer ▬ than ▪.

○ the ▬ is shorter so she needs more ▬ than ▪.

○ the ▬ is the same length as the ▪, so she needs the same number.

5. Choose two different measuring tools to measure the length of an object. Draw the object. Draw to show how many of each measuring tool below the object. Describe how and why the measurements are different.

Module 17 Assessment

Vocabulary

1. Circle the piece of string that is the same **length** as the spoon. Explain how you got your answer.

_____

Concepts and Skills

2. Circle the ribbon that is about 2 ▪ long. ◆ TEKS 1.7.B, 1.7.D

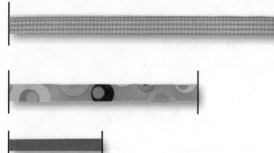

3. Draw a pencil that is about
5 ⬭ long. ◆ TEKS 1.7.B, 1.7.D

Choose the correct answer.

4. Which piece of yarn is longer than the pencil? ⬇ TEKS 1.7.A

○

○

○

5. Use ▪ and real objects. Which object is about 3 ▪ long?
⬇ TEKS 1.7.B, 1.7.D

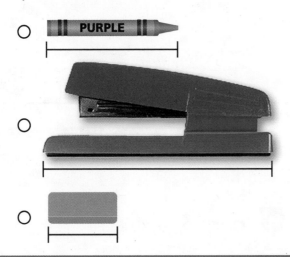

○ PURPLE

○

○

6. Which unit would you use the most of when measuring the same object? ⬇ TEKS 1.7.C

○ ◯ ○ _____ ○ ORANGE ▶

7. Which ribbon is shorter than the crayon? ⬇ TEKS 1.7.A

Green

○

○

○

Name _____

18.1 Time to the Hour

 Essential Question

How do you tell time to the hour?

Explore

Start at 1.
Write the unknown numbers.

Start

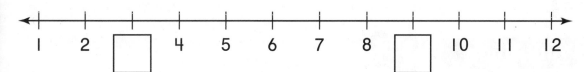

1   2   ☐   4   5   6   7   8   ☐   10   11   12

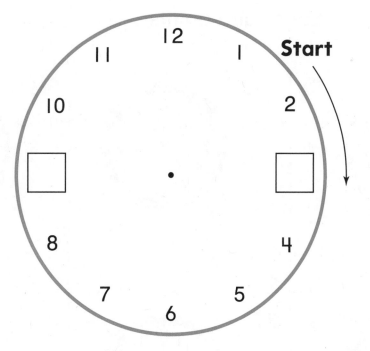

Start

Math Talk
Mathematical Processes

How are a clock face
and ordering numbers
alike? **Explain.**

FOR THE TEACHER • Have children look at the
number line and the clock face to decide which
numbers come after 2 and 8.

Module 18

Model and Draw

What does this clock show?

The **hour hand** points to the 3.
The minute hand points to 12.
It is 3 o'clock.

Say three o'clock.

Write 3:00 .

Share and Show

MATH BOARD

Look at where the hour hand points.
Write the time.

1.

_____

2.

_____

3.

_____

4.

_____

☑ 5.

_____

☑ 6.

_____

Problem Solving

Look at where the hour hand points.
Write the time.

7.

_____

8.

_____

9.

_____

10. **H.O.T.** Which time is **not** the same?
Circle it.

   1:00   1 o'clock

11. **H.O.T.** **Multi-Step** Morgan leaves for
school at 8 o'clock. Write and draw to
show 8 o'clock.

_____

Mathematical Processes
Model • Reason • Communicate

Choose the correct answer.

12. What time does the clock show?

○ 9:00   ○ 8:00   ○ 6:00

13. Which clock shows 3 o'clock?

○    ○    ○

14. On Jody's clock, the hour hand points to the 10. Which shows Jody's clock?

○    ○    ○

15. ⭐ **TEXAS Test Prep** What time does the clock show?

○ 12:00   ○ 2:00   ○ I o'clock

TAKE HOME ACTIVITY • Have your child describe what he or she did in this lesson.

Name _____

18.1 Time to the Hour

Look at where the hour hand points.
Write the time.

1.

_____

2.

_____

3.

_____

4.

_____

5.

_____

6.

_____

Problem Solving Real World

7. Multi-Step Suzanne eats dinner at 5 o'clock. Write and draw to show 5 o'clock.

_____

Choose the correct answer.

8. The clock shows the time Matt gets up in the morning. What time does the clock show?

○ 8:00   ○ 7:00   ○ 9:00

9. Which clock shows 6 o'clock?

○    ○    ○

10. Look at the hour hand. What is the time?

○ 4:00   ○ 9 o'clock   ○ 10:00

11. What time does the clock show?

○ 3 o'clock   ○ 2:00   ○ 5:00

TEKS Geometry and Measurement—1.7.E

MATHEMATICAL PROCESSES
1.1.A, 1.1.C, 1.1.D

 18.2 **Time to the Half Hour**

 Essential Question

How do you tell time to the half hour?

Explore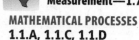

Circle **4:00**, **5:00**, or **between 4:00 and 5:00** to describe the time shown on the clock.

4:00

between 4:00 and 5:00

5:00

4:00

between 4:00 and 5:00

5:00

4:00

between 4:00 and 5:00

5:00

Math Talk
Mathematical Processes

Use **before** and **after** to **describe** the time shown on the middle clock.

 FOR THE TEACHER • Have children look at the hour hand on each clock to decide which choice best describes the time shown.

Model and Draw

As an **hour** passes, the hour hand
moves from one number
to the next number.
The minute hand points to 12.

When a **half hour** has passed,
the hour hand points halfway
between two numbers.
The minute hand points to 6.

The hour hand
is halfway between
the 7 and the 8.

half past 7:00

Share and Show

Look at where the hour hand points.
Write the time.

1.

_____

- - - - - - - - - - - -

_____

2.

_____

- - - - - - - - - - - -

_____

☑ 3.

_____

- - - - - - - - - - - -

_____

☑ 4.

_____

- - - - - - - - - - - -

_____

Name _____

Problem Solving

Write the time.

5.

_____

- - - - - - - - - - - - - - - -

_____

6.

_____

- - - - - - - - - - - - - - - -

_____

7. **H.O.T.** Tim plays soccer at half past 9:00. He eats lunch at half past 1:00. He sees a movie at half past 2:00.

Look at the clock.
Write what Tim does.

_____

- -

Tim

8. **H.O.T.** **Multi-Step** Tyra has a piano lesson at 5:00. The lesson ends at half past 5:00. How much time is Tyra at her lesson? Circle your answer.

half hour

hour

Choose the correct answer.

9. The game starts at the time shown on the clock. What time does the clock show?

- ○ half past 4
- ○ half past 5
- ○ half past 3

10. Which clock shows half past 7?

 ○

○

○

11. Jeff starts reading at 8:30. Which shows the time Jeff starts reading?

- ○ half past 7
- ○ half past 8
- ○ half past 9

12. ⭐ **TEXAS Test Prep** What time does the clock show?

- ○ 5:00
- ○ half past 4:00
- ○ 4:00

 TAKE HOME ACTIVITY • Say a time, such as half past 10:00. Ask your child to describe where the hour hand points at this time.

18.2 Time to the Half Hour

Look at where the hour hand points.
Write the time.

1.

_____

- - - - - - - - - - - - - - - - -

_____

2.

_____

- - - - - - - - - - - - - - - - -

_____

Problem Solving

3. Kenny wakes up at 8:00.
   He visits a friend at
   half past 10:00. He goes
   to the playground at 1:00.

   Look at the clock. Write what
   Kenny does.

_____

Kenny -

_____

Choose the correct answer.

4. The concert starts at the time shown on the clock. What time does the clock show?

○ half past 7:00

○ half past 8:00

○ half past 6:00

5. Which clock shows half past 3?

○    ○    ○

6. What is the time?

○ half past 10:00

○ half past 9:00

○ 9:00

7. **Multi-Step** Alex starts eating at 5:00. One half hour passes. What time does he stop eating?

○ half past 4:00   ○ half past 5:00   ○ half past 6:00

 **TEKS** Geometry and Measurement—1.7.E
MATHEMATICAL PROCESSES
1.1.A, 1.1.C, 1.1.D

18.3 Time to the Hour and Half Hour

? Essential Question

How are the minute hand and hour hand different for time to the hour and time to the half hour?

Explore

Each clock has an hour hand and a minute hand.
Use what you know about the hour hand to
write the unknown numbers.

It is 1:00.

The hour hand points to the _____.

The minute hand points

to the _____.

It is half past 1:00.

The hour hand points between

the _____ and the _____.

The minute hand points to the _____.

 FOR THE TEACHER • Have children look
at the two clocks and tell how much time
has passed.

 **Math Talk**
Mathematical Processes
Look at the top clock.
Explain how you know
which is the minute
hand.

An hour has 60 **minutes**.

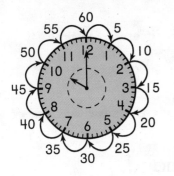

The clocks show 10:00.

A half hour has 30 minutes.

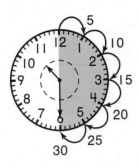

The clocks show half past 10:00. The **minute hand** has moved from the 12 to the 6.

Share and Show

Write the time.

1.

✓2.

✓3.

Name _____

Problem Solving

Write the time.

4.

5.

6.

Circle your answer.

7. Sara goes to the park when both the hour hand and the minute hand point to the 12. What time does Sara go to the park?

I o'clock   12 o'clock   2 o'clock

8. **H.O.T.** Mel goes to the park at half past 3. Which time shows when Mel goes to the park?

3:00   6:00   3:30

9. **H.O.T.** **Multi-Step** The hour hand points halfway between the 2 and 3. Draw the hour hand and the minute hand. Write the time.

Daily Assessment Task

Choose the correct answer.

10. The clock shows the time that Keri gets home from her soccer game. What time does the clock show?

○ 7:00   ○ 7:30   ○ 8:00

---

11. Which clock shows 11:30?

 ○    ○    ○

---

12. Sean goes to the library when the hour hand points to the 6, and the minute hand points to the 12. What time does Sean go to the library?

○ 6:00   ○ 6:30   ○ 7:30

---

13. ⭐ **TEXAS Test Prep**   What time is it?

○ 6:30   ○ 7:30   ○ 8:00

TAKE HOME ACTIVITY • At times on the half hour, have your child show you the minute hand and the hour hand on a clock, and tell what time it is.

Name _____

18.3 Time to the Hour and Half Hour

Write the time.

1.

2.

3.

Problem Solving Real World

Circle your answer.

4. Luis goes bowling at 11:00. Which time shows when Luis goes bowling?

   11 o'clock   12 o'clock   2 o'clock

5. **Multi-Step** The hour hand points halfway between 8 and 9. Draw the hour hand and the minute hand. Write the time.

Choose the correct answer.

6. The clock shows the time that Ken gets home from his karate lesson. What time does the clock show?

○ 7:30   ○ 8:30   ○ 8:00

7. Which clock shows 10:30?

○    ○    ○

8. What time is it?

○ 5:00   ○ 4:30   ○ 5:30

9. Sara goes to the park when the hour hand points to the 11, and the minute hand points to the 12. What time does Sara go to the park?

○ 11:00   ○ 12:00   ○ 11:30

18.4 Practice Time to the Hour and Half Hour

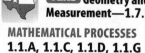 **TEKS** Geometry and Measurement—1.7.E

MATHEMATICAL PROCESSES
1.1.A, 1.1.C, 1.1.D, 1.1.G

? Essential Question

How do you know whether to draw and write time to the hour or half hour?

Explore Real World

Circle the clock that matches the problem.

FOR THE TEACHER • Read the following problems. Barbara goes to the store at 8:00. Circle the clock that shows 8:00. Children use the top work space to solve. Then have children solve this problem: Barbara takes Ria for a walk at 1:30. Circle the clock that shows 1:30.

Math Talk
Mathematical Processes

Describe how you know which clock shows 1:30.

Where should you draw the
minute hand to show the time?

Share and Show

Use the hour hand to write the time.
Draw the minute hand.

1.

2.

3.

4.

☑ 5.

☑ 6.

Name _____

Problem Solving

Use the hour hand to write the time.
Draw the minute hand.

7.

8.

9.

10. **H.O.T.** **What is the error?**
Zoey tried to show 6:00. Explain
how to change the clock to
show 6:00.

_____

_____

_____

_____

_____

11. **H.O.T.** **Multi-Step** Brandon has lunch at
1 o'clock. Which number does the hour hand
point to? Draw the hour hand. Which number
does the minute hand point to? Draw the
minute hand.

Choose the correct answer.

12. Sophia and Alana can go on a ride at 4:00. Which clock shows 4:00?

○    ○ 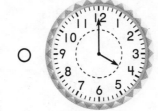   ○

13. What time is shown on the clock?

○ 1:00   ○ 12:30   ○ 1:30

14. Multi-Step Marybeth draws the clock to show 6:30. What number tells where the minute hand should point? Explain how you know.

_____

_ _

_____

15. ⭐ **TEXAS Test Prep** Which clock shows 11:30?

○    ○    ○

 TAKE HOME ACTIVITY • Show your child the time on a clock to the hour or half hour. Ask him or her to tell you what time is shown.

Name _____

18.4 Practice Time to the Hour and Half Hour

Use the hour hand to write the time.
Draw the minute hand.

1.

2.

3.

Problem Solving

4. **What is the error?** Russ tried to show 9:30. Explain how to change the clock to show 9:30.

_____

_____

_____

_____

Choose the correct answer.

5. Gina and Sean go to the movies at 7:00.
   Which clock shows 7:00?

○    ○    ○

6. What time is shown on the clock?

○ 9:00   ○ 10:30   ○ 9:30

7. Which clock shows 2:30?

○    ○    ○

8. **Multi-Step** Lizzy draws the clock to show
   4:30. What number tells where the minute
   hand should point?

○ 6   ○ 12   ○ 9

© Houghton Mifflin Harcourt Publishing Company

Module 18 Assessment

Vocabulary

Circle the clock that shows time to the **half hour**. (p. 624)
Underline the clock that shows time to the **hour**. (p. 624)

1.

Concepts and Skills

Write the time. ✦TEKS 1.7.E

2.

_____

3.

_____
- - - - - - - - - - - - - - - -

Write the time. ✦TEKS 1.7.E

4.

5.

Choose the correct answer.

6. What is the time? ⬐ TEKS 1.7.E

- ○ 7:00
- ○ half past 7:00
- ○ 8:00

---

7. What time is it? ⬐ TEKS 1.7.E

- ○ 8:00
- ○ 9 o'clock
- ○ 10 o'clock

---

8. Which clock shows 12:30? ⬐ TEKS 1.7.E

○  ○ ○

---

9. Which clock shows 10:00? ⬐ TEKS 1.7.E

○  ○ ○

✓ **Unit 4 Assessment**

Vocabulary

Write the words that describe the shape. (p. 572)

1.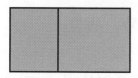

_____

2.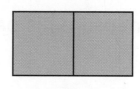

_____

| equal parts |
| unequal parts |

Concepts and Skills

3. Circle the shapes that can combine to make the new shape. �’ TEKS 1.6.F

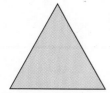 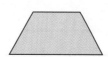

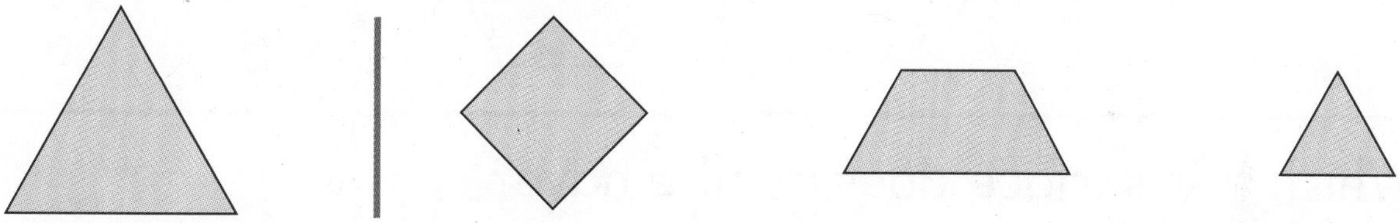

4. Draw a line under the objects that have both flat and curved surfaces. �’ TEKS 1.6.E

5. Draw lines to show 2 equal parts. �’ TEKS 1.6.G, 1.6.H

 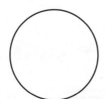 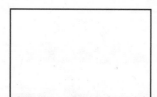 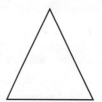

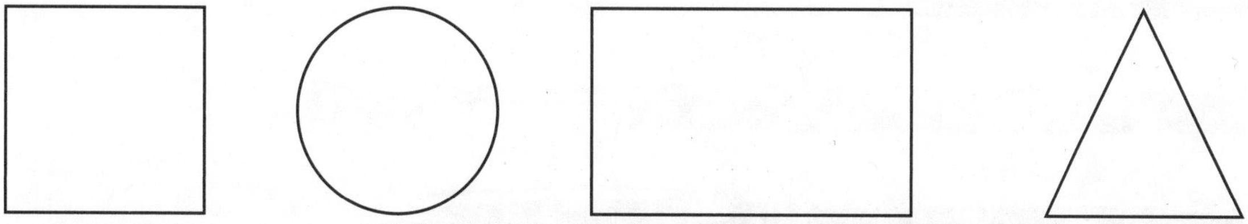

Choose the correct answer.

6. Which shading shows a fourth of a rectangle? 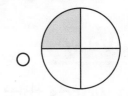 TEKS 1.6.G, 1.6.H

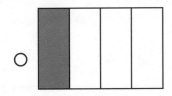 ○

 ○

○

7. Mike uses 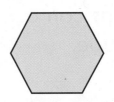 to measure his pencil. About how long is the pencil? TEKS 1.7.B, 1.7.D

○ about 4 ⬭

○ about 6 ⬭

○ about 2 ⬭

8. How many vertices does a hexagon have? TEKS 1.6.D

○ 4

○ 6

○ 5

9. Which flat surface does a cube have? TEKS 1.6.E

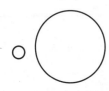 ○

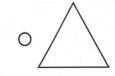 ○

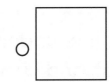 ○

10. A box is the same length as this string. Use string to find which object will fit in the box.

○

○

○

Choose the correct answer.

11. What is the time? 📍 TEKS 1.7.E

- ○ 10 o'clock
- ○ 4 o'clock
- ○ 12 o'clock

12. Which shows halves? 📍 TEKS 1.6.G, 1.6.H

 ○ ○ ○

13. What time is it? 📍 TEKS 1.7.E

- ○ 6 o'clock
- ○ half past 12
- ○ 12 o'clock

14. Which solid has 9 edges? 📍 TEKS 1.6.E

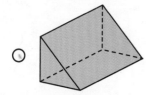 ○ 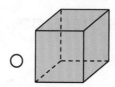 ○ 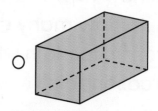 ○

15. Why does the straw use fewer units to measure? 📍 TEKS 1.7.C

- ○ the straw is shorter so it uses more units
- ○ the straw is longer so it uses fewer units
- ○ the straw is the same length so it uses the same number of units

16. Which solid matches the riddle?  TEKS 1.6.E

> I am a block.
> I have 6 faces that
> are squares.

○   ○   ○

17. Use the following clues to draw a shape.

- The shape has only straight sides.
- The shape has more than 3 sides.
- The shape has fewer than 5 corners.
- The shape can be cut into fourths.

- What information am I given?
- What is my plan or strategy?
- How can I solve?
- How can I check my answer?

Draw to show the shape. Draw lines to show how the shape can be cut. Write how many equal shares there are. Justify. Explain why your answer is reasonable. TEKS 1.6.A, 1.6.D, 1.6.G

What shapes are the equal shares?

_____

How many corners does one equal share have?

_____

Data Analysis

Show What You Know ✓

Check your understanding of important skills.

Name _____

Make a Concrete Graph

Sort a handful of ▪ and ▫. Make a concrete graph.

Square Colors						

1. How many ▪ are there? _____

More, Fewer

2. Color the squares to show a set of fewer.

🚗	🚗	🚗	🚗	

Draw Equal Groups

3. Draw a ◯ below each picture to show
the same number of objects.

✿	✿	✿		

FAMILY NOTE: This page checks your child's understanding of important skills needed for success in Unit 5.

Assessment Options:
Soar to Success Math

Vocabulary Builder

Review Words

graph
more
fewer
most
fewest

Visualize It

Complete the chart.
Mark each row with a ✔.

Word	I Know	Sounds Familiar	I Do Not Know
graph			
more			
fewer			
most			
fewest			

Understand Vocabulary

Use the review words. Label the groups.

1.

_____   _____

2.

_____   _____

GO DIGITAL
• Interactive Student Edition
• Multimedia eGlossary

Rain, Rain, Go Away

written by Tim Johnson

This Take-Home Book belongs to

_____

Reading and Writing Math

This take-home book will help you preview graphing.

MATHEMATICAL PROCESSES 1.1.A, 1.1.D

It seemed like it had been raining for weeks.

"Let's keep track of the weather over the next 15 days of school," said Ms. Parks.

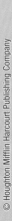

The students took turns making tally marks.

At the end of **15** days, they looked at their work.

How many school days were sunny?
Count the tally marks.
How many were cloudy?
Write the numbers.
Were there more sunny or more
cloudy days?

How many days were not windy?
How many were windy?
Which side of the chart has more
tally marks?
Write the numbers.

How many days were warm?
How many were cool?
Were there fewer warm days or fewer
cool days?

Wet   Dry

11   4

11 days were rainy, wet days.

4 of the days were dry, with no rain at all.

Draw the tally marks.

Today is _____, _____

and _____.

Draw a picture of today's weather.
Below the picture write three words
that describe the weather.

Name _____

Write about the Math

Write Math Look at the tally chart. Draw a picture to show which kind of day you like. Then write questions about the tally chart.

_____

- -

_____

- -

_____

- -

_____

- -

_____

- -

How Many Tally Marks?

Use the tally chart to answer each question.

1. How many days were sunny? _____

2. How many days were rainy? _____

3. Were there fewer sunny days or fewer rainy days? Explain.

_____

_ _

_____

4. How many more days were sunny than rainy?

_____ more sunny days

MATH BOARD Make your own tally chart. Ask 10 classmates if they like hot or cold days. Then ask a classmate questions about your tally chart.

TEKS Data Analysis—
1.8.C
MATHEMATICAL PROCESSES
1.1.A, 1.1.D, 1.1.E, 1.1.G

19.1 Read Picture Graphs

? Essential Question

What do the pictures in a picture graph show?

Explore

Use . Draw to show the cubes.
Write how many more .

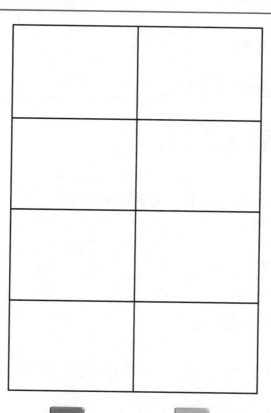

_____ more 🟥

Math Talk
Mathematical Processes
Describe how you can use your picture to compare the cubes.

 FOR THE TEACHER • Read the following problem. There are 2 green cubes and 4 blue cubes. How many more blue cubes are there than green cubes?

Module 19

Children at the Playground					
⚘ swings	☺	☺	☺	☺	
⚘ slide	☺	☺			

A **picture graph** uses pictures to show information.

Each ☺ stands for 1 child.

There are _____ children on the ⚘.

There are _____ children on the ⚘.

There are more children on the _____.

Share and Show MATH BOARD

Our Favorite Activity at the Fair							
animals	☺	☺	☺	☺	☺		
⚙ rides	☺	☺	☺	☺	☺	☺	☺

Each ☺ stands for 1 child.

Use the picture graph to answer the questions.

1. Which activity did more children choose? Circle your answer.

2. How many children chose ?   _____ children

☑3. How many children chose ⚙?   _____ children

☑4. How many fewer children chose than ⚙?   _____ fewer children

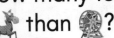 **660** six hundred sixty

Name _____

Problem Solving

What We Drink for Lunch										
🥛 milk	�	☺	☺	☺	☺	☺	☺	☺		
🧃 juice	☺	☺	☺							
💧 water	☺	☺	☺	☺	☺					

Each  ☺ stands for 1 child.

Use the picture graph to answer the questions.

5. How many children drink 🥛?

_____ children

6. How many children in all drink 🧃 and 💧?

_____ children

7. How many fewer children drink 💧 than 🥛?

_____ fewer children

8. How many more children drink 🥛 than 🧃?

_____ more children

9. **H.O.T.** How many children in all drink 🥛, 🧃, and 💧?

_____ children

10. **H.O.T.** Multi-Step 4 new children join the class. They drink 🧃 at lunch. Now, how many more children drink 🧃 than 💧?

_____ more children

Module 19 • Lesson 1

six hundred sixty-one **661**

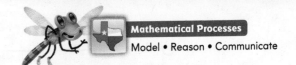

Our Favorite Animal at the Zoo

🦓	zebras	🧍	🧍	🧍	🧍	🧍			
🦁	lions	🧍	🧍	🧍	🧍	🧍	🧍	🧍	🧍
🦭	seals	🧍							

Each 🧍 stands for 1 child.

Choose the correct answer.

11. How many children chose
🦓 and 🦭 altogether?

- ○ 5 children
- ○ 1 child
- ○ 6 children

12. Apply How many more children
chose 🦁 than 🦭?

- ○ 7 children
- ○ 8 children
- ○ 1 child

13. Multi-Step How many more children
chose 🦁 than 🦓 and 🦭
altogether?

- ○ 8 children
- ○ 2 children
- ○ 6 children

14. ⭐ **TEXAS Test Prep** Use the graph at
the top. How many children chose 🦁?

- ○ 8 children   ○ 9 children   ○ 1 child

TAKE HOME ACTIVITY • Keep track of the weather for one week by drawing
a picture each day to show if it is sunny, cloudy, or rainy. At the end of the week,
ask your child what the weather was like for most of the week.

TEKS Data Analysis—1.8.C
MATHEMATICAL PROCESSES 1.1.A, 1.1.D, 1.1.E, 1.1.G

Name ____________________

19.1 Read Picture Graphs

How We Go to School
car
bicycle
bus

Each  stands for 1 child.

Use the picture graph to answer the questions.

1. How many children go by ? ____ children

2. How many children go by ? ____ children

3. Which way do most children go to school? ____________

Problem Solving Real World

4. How many more children go by car than bus? ____ more children

5. How many children go by , , and 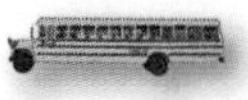 altogether? ____ children

What We Collect

🪙🪙🪙 coins	👤	👤	👤	👤				
🖼 sports cards	👤	👤	👤	👤	👤	👤	👤	
✨ stickers	👤	👤	👤	👤	👤			

Each 👤 stands for 1 child.

Choose the correct answer.

6. How many children collect
   🪙🪙🪙 and ✨ altogether?

   ○ 5
   ○ 2
   ○ 9

7. How many fewer children
   collect ✨ than 🖼?

   ○ 2
   ○ 5
   ○ 7

8. How many more children
   collect ✨ than 🪙🪙🪙?

   ○ 7
   ○ 1
   ○ 4

9. **Multi-Step** How many more children
   collect 🪙🪙🪙 and 🖼 altogether
   than ✨?

   ○ 2
   ○ 5
   ○ 6

19.2
HANDS ON

Make Picture Graphs

 **TEKS** Data Analysis—
1.8.A, 1.8.B
Also 1.8.C
MATHEMATICAL PROCESSES
1.1.A, 1.1.D, 1.1.E, 1.1.G

? Essential Question

How do you make a picture graph to answer a question?

Explore Real World

Use ● to solve the problem.
Draw to show your work.

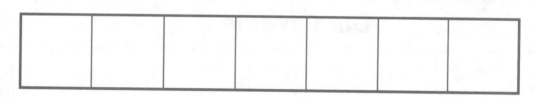

Which has more?

Math Talk
Mathematical Processes

Describe what the picture graph shows.

FOR THE TEACHER • Read the following problem. Asaf has 6 baseballs. He has 4 bats. Does he have more baseballs or bats? Have children draw circles to show the baseballs and bats. Then have them circle the object with more.

Model and Draw

Are there more black or white sheep in the picture? Make a picture graph to find out.

Sheep in the Meadow

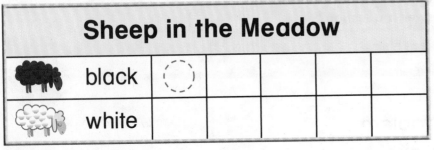 black	○					
white						

Each ○ stands for 1 sheep.

There are more _____ sheep.

Share and Show

 MATH BOARD

Do more children like cats or dogs?
Ask 10 friends which pet they like better.
Draw 1 circle for each child's answer.

Our Favorite Pet

cats										
dogs										

Each ○ stands for 1 child.

Use the picture graph to answer the questions.

1. How many children chose ? _____ children

☑ 2. How many children chose ? _____ children

☑ 3. Which pet did more children choose? Circle your answer.

Name _____

Problem Solving

Which activity do the most children like best?
Ask 10 friends. Draw I circle for each child's answer.

Our Favorite Activity									
reading									
computer									
sports									

Each ◯ stands for I child.

Use the picture graph to answer the questions.

4. How many children chose ?

_____ children

5. How many children chose 🖥 and ⚽?

_____ children

6. Which activity did the most children choose? Circle it.

7. Did all your classmates make picture graphs that look the same? Circle **yes** or **no**.

8. **H.O.T.** Write your own question about the graph.

_____

9. **H.O.T.** **Multi-Step** Look at the question you wrote. Answer your question.

_____

Matt made this picture graph to show the paint colors his friends like best.

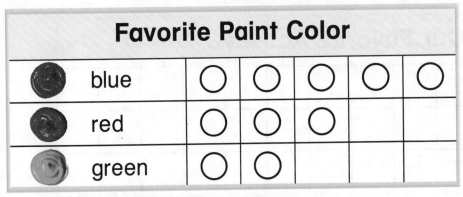

Favorite Paint Color

	blue	◯	◯	◯	◯	◯
	red	◯	◯	◯		
	green	◯	◯			

Each ◯ stands for 1 child.

Choose the correct answer.

10. Apply How many children chose a paint color?

○ 9   ○ 5   ○ 10

11. How many fewer children chose than ⬤ ?

○ 3   ○ 7   ○ 2

12. Multi-Step Matt adds his own choice to the graph. Now, two colors have the same number of circles. Which color did Matt choose?

○   ○   ○

13. ⭐ **TEXAS Test Prep** Use the graph at the top. How many children chose ⬤ and ⬤ ?

○ 8
○ 3
○ 5

 TAKE HOME ACTIVITY • Ask your child to make a picture graph showing how many glasses of water each family member drinks in a day. Discuss how to find who drinks the most water.

Name _____

19.2
HANDS ON

Make Picture Graphs

Do more people like morning or evening?
Ask 10 friends or family members which they like
better. Draw 1 circle for each person's answer.

Our Favorite Time of Day

morning							
evening							

Each ◯ stands for 1 person.

Use the picture graph to answer the questions.

1. How many people chose ?   _____ people

_____

2. How many people chose ?   _____ people

Problem Solving **Real World**

3. Which time of day did more people
   choose? Explain how you know.

_____

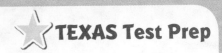
Marley made this picture graph to show the instrument the class likes best.

Our Favorite Instrument						
🥁 drum	◯	◯	◯	◯	◯	
△ triangle	◯	◯	◯	◯		
🔔 bell	◯	◯	◯			

Each ◯ stands for 1 child.

Choose the correct answer.

4. How many children chose a favorite instrument?

  ○ 11   ○ 12   ○ 3

5. How many fewer children chose 🔔 than △?

  ○ 2   ○ 3   ○ 1

6. **Multi-step** Marley likes 🥁 the best. He adds his own choice to the graph. Now, how many fewer children choose 🔔 than 🥁?

  ○ 3   ○ 4   ○ 1

7. How many children chose 🔔 and △ altogether?

  ○ 8   ○ 7   ○ 3

670 six hundred seventy

Name _____

19.3 Read Bar Graphs

? Essential Question

How can you read a bar graph to find the number that a bar shows?

Explore Real World

Hands On

Write a question about the graph.
Use ⬤ to help solve the problem.

Type of Sneaker We Are Wearing											
laces	◯	◯	◯	◯	◯	◯	◯	◯	◯	◯	
👟 no laces	◯	◯	◯	◯	◯	◯					

Each ◯ stands for 1 child.

_____
_____
_____
_____
_____
_____
_____

FOR THE TEACHER • Read the following problem. Emma's class made this picture graph. What question could Emma's class answer using the graph? Write the question and the answer.

Math Talk
Mathematical Processes

Describe how the class made this picture graph.

Model and Draw

In a **bar graph**, each bar shows information. You can compare the lengths of the bars.
What title describes this graph?

> Touch the end of a bar. Look down to see the number of children.

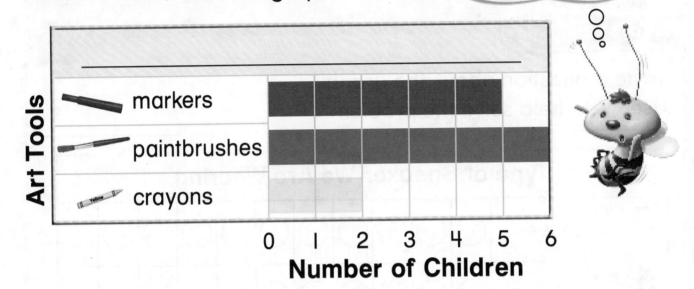

Art Tools

markers
paintbrushes
crayons

0 1 2 3 4 5 6
Number of Children

Share and Show

MATH BOARD

Use the bar graph to answer the questions.

1. How many children chose ?

_____ children

2. How many children chose ▱ Yellow ▱?

_____ children

3. How many more children chose ▬▬ than ▱ Yellow ▱?

_____ more children

✓4. Which art tool did the fewest children choose? Circle it.

✓5. Which art tool did the most children choose? Circle it.

Name _____

Problem Solving

Use the bar graph to answer the questions.

6. How many children chose ?

    _____ children

7. How many children chose  ?

    _____ children

8. How many children in all chose and  ?

    _____ children

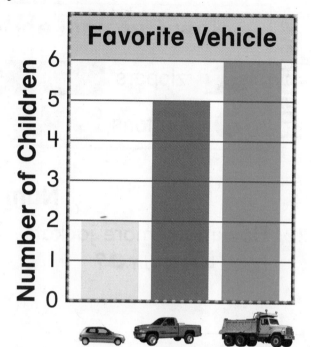

9. Use the bar graph to write a new question.

    _____

10. **H.O.T.** Order the vehicles from least to most votes. Write 1 for the least votes and 3 for the most votes.

    _____   _____   _____

11. **H.O.T.** **Multi-Step** If one more child chose , then how many more children chose  than ?

    _____ more children

Mathematical Processes
Model • Reason • Communicate

Choose the correct answer.

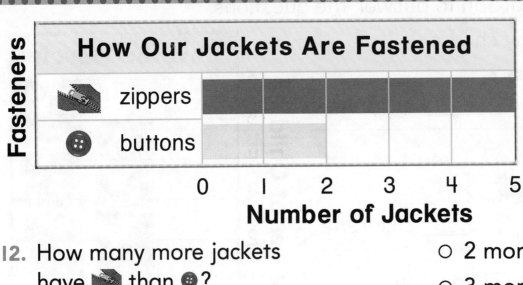

Fasteners

How Our Jackets Are Fastened						
zippers						
buttons						

0   1   2   3   4   5
Number of Jackets

12. How many more jackets have 🤐 than 🔘?
   - ○ 2 more jackets
   - ○ 3 more jackets
   - ○ 5 more jackets

13. Kim puts on a jacket with 🔘. Add her jacket to the graph. Now how many jackets have 🔘?
   - ○ 4 jackets
   - ○ 5 jackets
   - ○ 3 jackets

14. **Record** Ed adds a row to the graph to show jackets with snaps. 2 fewer jackets have snaps than have zippers. How many jackets have snaps?
   - ○ 3 jackets
   - ○ 1 jackets
   - ○ 2 jackets

15. ⭐ **TEXAS Test Prep** Use the bar graph at the top. How many jackets have 🤐?
   - ○ 2 jackets
   - ○ 7 jackets
   - ○ 5 jackets

TAKE HOME ACTIVITY • Have your child look through newspapers and magazines for examples of bar graphs. Talk about what information is shown in each graph you find.

19.3 Read Bar Graphs

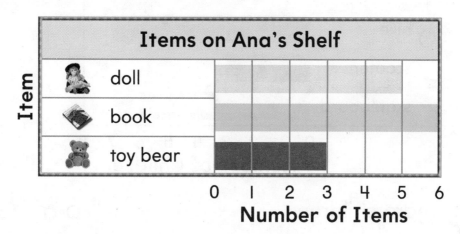

Items on Ana's Shelf

Use the bar graph to answer the questions.

1. How many are there?

    ____

2. How many are there?

    ____

3. How many more are there than ?

    ____ more

Problem Solving Real World

4. Which item does Ana have the fewest of? Circle it.

5. Which item does Ana have the most of? Circle it.

Choose the correct answer.

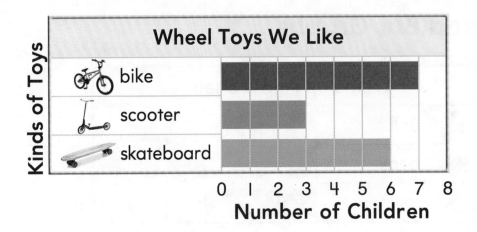

6. How many more children chose 🚲 than 🛴?

○ 6
○ 3
○ 4

7. Another child chooses 🛹. How many children chose 🛹 now?

○ 8
○ 6
○ 7

8. Keshawn adds a row to the graph to show 🛼. 2 fewer children like 🛼 than 🛴. How many children like 🛼?

○ 1
○ 3
○ 2

9. **Multi-Step** If 2 more children chose 🛴, then how many more children chose 🚲 than 🛴?

○ 1
○ 2
○ 3

Name _____

19.4
HANDS ON

Make Bar Graphs

? **Essential Question**

How does a bar graph help you compare information?

Explore

Hands On

Use ▣ to model the problem.
Color 1 box for each food item
to complete the graph.

Kinds of Food	Food Sold at the Soccer Game							
🍕 pizza								
🌭 hot dogs								
🌮 tacos								

0 1 2 3 4 5 6 7
Number of Food Items Sold

Math Talk
Mathematical Processes

How do you know
that you counted each
food in the picture?
Explain.

FOR THE TEACHER • Read the following
problem. Dan keeps track of the food he sells
at the soccer game. He sells all of the food on
the table. Make a bar graph to show the food
Dan sells.

Are there more or 🌻 in the garden?
Make a bar graph to find out.
Color I box for each flower in the picture.

	Flowers in the Garden							
🌼 daisies								
🌻 sunflowers								

Kinds of Flowers

0 I 2 3 4 5 6 7
Number of Flowers

There are more _____ in the garden.

Share and Show

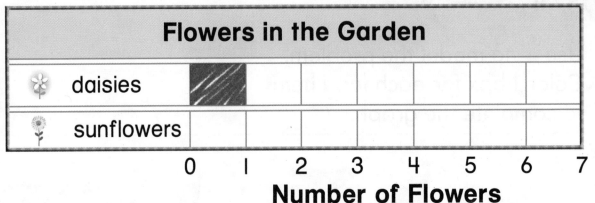

Do more children write with their left hand or
right hand? Ask 10 friends which hand they use.
Make a bar graph.

	Hand We Use to Write									
✋ left										
✋ right										

Writing Hand

0 I 2 3 4 5 6 7 8 9 10
Number of Children

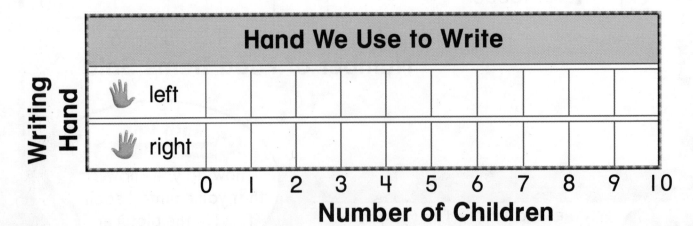

I. Which hand do more children use to write? _____

Name _____

Do children like , , or ⬤ best?
Ask 10 friends which toy they like best.

2. Make a bar graph. Write a title and labels for your graph.

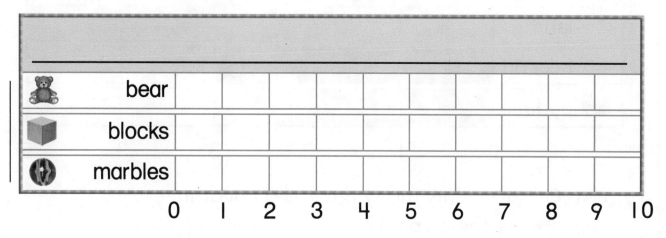

	bear										
blocks										
marbles										

0   1   2   3   4   5   6   7   8   9   10

_____

3. Which toy did the most children choose? Circle it.

4. How many children chose ?

_____ children

5. **H.O.T.** How are picture graphs and bar graphs alike?

Math on the Spot

_____

_____

6. **H.O.T. Multi-Step** Explain what would happen if you added another toy to your graph.

_____

_____

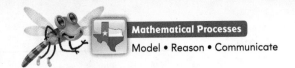

Mathematical Processes
Model • Reason • Communicate

Choose the correct answer.

Tom's class made this bar graph.
Use the bar graph to answer the questions.

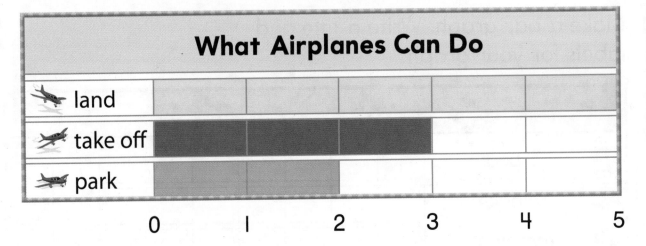

What Airplanes Can Do

	land					
take off					
park					
0	1	2	3	4	5

7. **Use Graphs** How many times did children
   see  at the airport?

   ○ 3   ○ 2   ○ 5

8. Which did the children see airplanes do the least?

   ○    ○    ○

9. Which did the children see airplanes do the most?

   ○    ○    ○

10. ⭐ **TEXAS Test Prep** Use the graph at the top.   ○ 5
    How many more children saw  than ?   ○ 1

                                                              ○ 3

TAKE HOME ACTIVITY • Your child has learned how to
make picture graphs and bar graphs. Ask your child to explain
how bar graphs are different from picture graphs.

TEKS Data Analysis—1.8.A, 1.8.B
Also 1.8.C
MATHEMATICAL PROCESSES 1.1.A, 1.1.D, 1.1.E, 1.1.G

Name ______________________________

19.4 Make Bar Graphs

HANDS ON

1. Which item do most people like to wear?
Ask 10 friends or family members.
Make a bar graph.

Favorite Item to Wear

Item							
hat							
glasses							
slippers							

0 1 2 3 4 5 6 7

Number of People

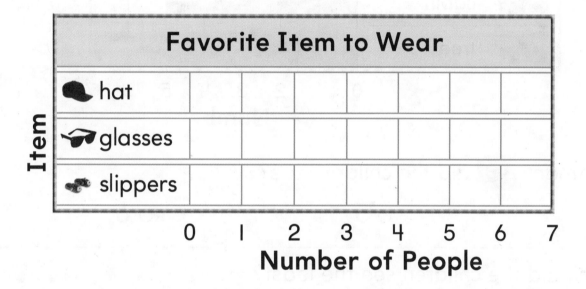

2. Which item do most people like? Circle it.

3. How many people like ?

____ people

4. **Multi-Step** How would you change your graph to show that 4 people like ? Explain.

____

____

Choose the correct answer.

The class made a graph.
Use the bar graph to answer the questions.

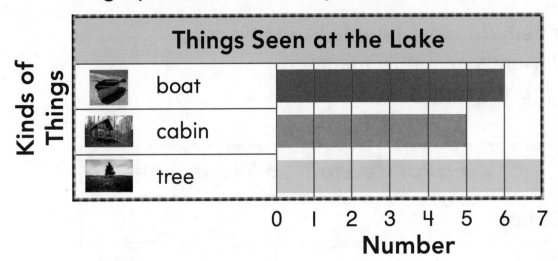

5. How many did the children see?

○ 7   ○ 5   ○ 6

6. Which did the children see the least?

○   ○   ○

7. Which did the children see the most?

○   ○   ○

8. How many more than did the children see?

○ 1   ○ 0   ○ 2

TEKS Data Analysis—
1.8.A

MATHEMATICAL PROCESSES
1.1.A, 1.1.D, 1.1.E, 1.1.G

19.5 Tally Marks

? Essential Question

How do you count the tallies on a T-chart?

Explore Real World

Hands On

Use ● to solve the problem.
Draw to show your work.
Write how many.

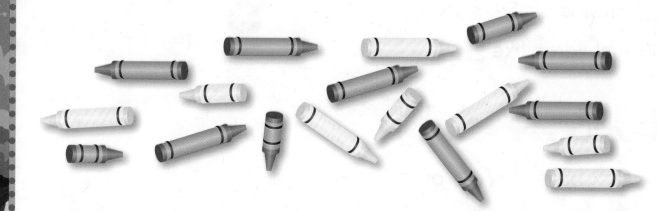

_____   _____

FOR THE TEACHER • Read the following problem. Jane is sorting her crayons. Draw to show how she can sort the crayons into two groups.

Math Talk
Mathematical Processes

Describe how you sorted the counters.

Model and Draw

Use the T-chart about food children like to answer the questions.

chicken	pizza
III	IIII III

Each **I** is a **tally mark**.
It stands for 1 child.
IIII stands for 5 children.

More children like _____.

You can use a **T-chart** to collect information.

Share and Show

MATH BOARD

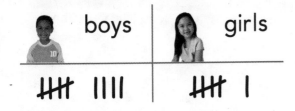

boys	girls
IIII IIII	IIII I

Use the T-chart about boys and girls in our class to answer the questions.

1. How many girls are in the class? _____ girls

2. How many boys are in the class? _____ boys

☑ 3. How many children are in the class in all? _____ children

☑ 4. Are there more boys or girls in the class? _____

Problem Solving

soccer	swimming
ⅢⅢ ‖	‖‖

Use the T-chart about which sports children like to answer the questions.

5. How many children chose ?   _____ children

6. How many children chose 🟤?   _____ children

7. How many more children chose
🟤 than 🟤?   _____ more children

8. Which sport did the most
children choose? Circle it.

9. **H.O.T.** Write your own question
about the T-chart.

_____

10. **H.O.T.** **Multi-Step** Sam asked some
other children which sport they like.
They all chose 🟤. Now the most
children chose 🟤. How many children
did Sam ask?   _____ children

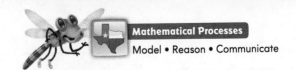

Daily Assessment Task

Choose the correct answer.

Use the T-chart about which season children like better to answer the questions.

winter	summer
ⅢⅡ I	ⅢⅡ IIII

11. **Use Diagrams** How many children chose ?

   ○ 5 children   ○ 9 children   ○ 6 children

12. How many children chose ❄ ?

   ○ 6 children   ○ 5 children   ○ 8 children

13. How many more children chose than ❄ ?

   ○ 6 children   ○ 9 children   ○ 3 children

14. ⭐ **TEXAS Test Prep** Which tally marks show the number 10?

   ○ ⅢⅡ   ○ ⅢⅡ ⅢⅡ   ○ ⅢⅡ ⅢⅡ ⅢⅡ

 TAKE HOME ACTIVITY • Together with your child, make a T-chart showing how many times the two of you say the word "eat" during a meal. Then have your child say the number.

19.5 Tally Marks

broccoli	carrots
卌 III	卌 II

Use the T-chart about vegetables children like to answer the questions.

1. How many children like ?   _____ children

2. How many more children like than ?   _____ more child

3. How many children in all eat and ?   _____ children

Problem Solving Real World

4. **Multi-Step** Brendan asked some more children which vegetable they like. 5 more children like . Now how many children like ?   _____ children

Choose the correct answer.

Use the T-chart about stickers children like to answer questions 5–7.

star stickers	happy stickers
̶H̶H̶I	̶H̶H̶I IIII

5. How many children like ?

○ 5   ○ 9   ○ 8

6. How many children like ?

○ 9   ○ 4   ○ 5

7. How many more children like than ?

○ 4   ○ 7   ○ 5

8. Which tally marks show the number 7?

○ ̶H̶H̶ I   ○ ̶H̶H̶ ̶H̶H̶   ○ ̶H̶H̶ II

Name _____

19.6 Make Tally Charts

HANDS ON

? **Essential Question**

Why is a tally chart a good way to show information that you have collected?

Explore

You can use a **tally chart** to collect information.
Complete the tally chart.

	Our Favorite Game		Total
	card game	⊞	
	board game	⊞ ⊞	

Use the tally chart to answer the questions.
Which game did the most children choose? Circle it.

Which game did the fewest children choose? Circle it.

Math Talk
Mathematical Processes

How do you know which game is the favorite? **Explain.**

FOR THE TEACHER • Read the following problem. Ava asks the children in her class which of two games they like the best. She makes a tally mark to show each child's answer. Which game did the most children choose? Which did the fewest children choose?

© Houghton Mifflin Harcourt Publishing Company

Model and Draw

How can you make a tally chart to show the boats at the lake?

Sort the boats.

Boats at the Lake		Total
boats with sails	⋮	
boats without sails		

Share and Show

Use the picture to complete the tally chart. Then answer the questions.

Fish in the Tank		Total
zebra fish		
angel fish		

1. How many are in the tank?

_____

2. How many more than are there?

_____ more

3. How many and are in the tank?

_____ fish

Name _____

Problem Solving

Which of these snacks do most children like the best? Ask 10 friends. Make 1 tally mark for each child's answer.

Collect data.

Our Favorite Snack		Total
pretzel		
apple		
yogurt		

Use the tally chart to answer the questions.

4. How many children chose 🥨?

_____ children

5. How many children chose ?

_____ children

6. Which snack do most children like best? Circle it.

7. **H.O.T.** What if 6 children out of the 10 chose 🥨? Which snack would be the favorite? Circle it.

Math on the Spot

8. **H.O.T.** Multi-Step Explain how you chose your answer in Exercise 7.

_____

_____

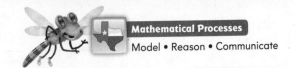

Daily Assessment Task

Jenna asked 10 friends to choose their favorite subject. Choose the correct answer.

Our Favorite School Subject		Total
math	卌 I	
reading	II	
science	II	

9. Which subject did the most children choose?

○ math   ○ reading   ○ science

10. **Use Graphs** How many more children chose math than reading?

○ 5 children   ○ 2 children   ○ 4 children

11. How many fewer children chose science than math?

○ 2 children   ○ 4 children   ○ 5 children

12. ⭐ **TEXAS Test Prep** Which fruit did the most children choose?

Fruit We Like		Total
🍎 apple	IIII	4
🍌 banana	卌	5
🍇 grapes	II	2

○

○

○

 TAKE HOME ACTIVITY • With your child, survey friends and family to find out their favorite foods. Draw tally marks to record the results, and then prepare the food.

19.6 Make Tally Charts

HANDS ON

Use the picture to complete the tally chart. Then answer the questions.

Shells Ben Found on the Beach		Total
🦪 clam		
🐚 scallop		
🐌 snail		

1. How many 🐚 did Ben find? _____ 🐚 shells

---

2. What if Ben found 4 more 🦪. Which shells would he have found the most of?

Problem Solving Real World

3. **Multi-Step** Explain how you chose your answer in Exercise 2.

_____

- - - - - - - - - - - - - -

_____

Choose the correct answer.

Maggie asked her friends and family to choose their favorite insects.

Insects We Like		Total
 ladybug	⊥⊥⊥⊥ ‖	7
grasshopper	‖	2
bumblebee	‖‖	3

4. Which insect did the fewest people choose?

○   ○   ○

5. How many more people chose  than  ?

○ 3   ○ 5   ○ 4

6. How many fewer people chose  than  ?

○ 1   ○ 2   ○ 3

7. Which insect did the most people choose?

○   ○   ○

Name _____

19.7 PROBLEM SOLVING • Represent Data

TEKS Data Analysis—
1.8.B, 1.8.C
Also 1.8A
MATHEMATICAL PROCESSES
1.1.A, 1.1.D, 1.1.E, 1.1.G

? **Essential Question**

How can showing information in a graph help you solve problems?

! Unlock the Problem

Brad sees many animals at the park. How can you find how many animals Brad sees?

Read	Plan
What information am I given?	**What is my plan or strategy?**
the number of <u>**rabbits**</u>, <u>**birds**</u>, and <u>**deer**</u> in the picture	I can _____ _____.

Solve

Show how you solve the problem.

Animals Brad Sees

Animals		0	1	2	3	4	5	6	7
	rabbit								
	bird								
	deer								

Number of Animals

_____ + _____ + _____ = _____ animals

HOME CONNECTION • Your child learned how to represent data from a picture in a bar graph. Have your child explain why it is easier to use data in a bar graph than in a picture.

© Houghton Mifflin Harcourt Publishing Company

Make a graph to solve.

1. Jake has 4 more train cars than Ed. Ed has 3 train cars. Ben has 2 fewer train cars than Ed. How many train cars does Jake have?

_____ train cars

Our Train Cars

Children									
Jake									
Ed									
Ben									

0　1　2　3　4　5　6　7　8
Number of Train Cars

2. Marla has 8 dolls. Three dolls have blue eyes. The rest have brown. How many dolls have brown eyes?

_____ dolls

Dolls Marla Has

Eye Color								
blue eyes								
brown eyes								

0　1　2　3　4　5　6　7　8
Number of Dolls

Math Talk
Mathematical Processes

Describe how the bar graph helps you solve Exercise 2.

Name _____

Find out about the eye color of your classmates.

✓3. Write a question you can ask your friends.

_____

✓4. Ask 10 friends your question. Make a tally chart.

Collect data.

	Total

Problem Solving

5. **H.O.T.** **Multi-Step** Use the tally chart in Exercise 4 to make a bar graph.

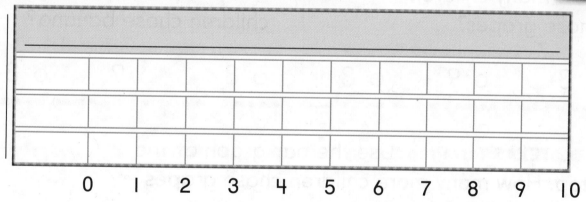

0 1 2 3 4 5 6 7 8 9 10

6. **H.O.T.** **Multi-Step** Use the bar graph to write a question. Then solve it.

_____

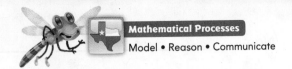

Daily Assessment Task

Choose the correct answer.

What is your favorite fruit? Nina asked 20 children this question. Then she made a bar graph. But Nina spilled paint on the graph.

Our Favorite Fruit

REMEMBER Nina asked 20 people.

7. How many children chose grapes?

○ 3   ○ 9   ○ 8

8. **Use Graphs** How many children chose banana?

○ 8   ○ 9   ○ 3

9. ⭐ **TEXAS Test Prep** Use the bar graph at the top. How many more children chose grapes than apple?

○ 3 more children   ○ 6 more children   ○ 9 more children

TAKE HOME ACTIVITY • Work with your child to make a tally chart and a bar graph showing the favorite color of 10 family members or friends. Talk about the results.

19.7 PROBLEM SOLVING •
Represent Data

Find out about the hair color of some friends.

1. Write a question you can ask your friends.

_____

2. Ask 10 friends your question. Make a tally chart.

		Total

Problem Solving Real World

Multi-Step Use the tally chart to make a bar graph.

0   1   2   3   4   5   6   7   8   9   10

_____

3. Use the bar graph to write a question.

_____

Choose the correct answer.

What is your favorite breakfast? Lily asked some friends this question. Then she made a bar graph.

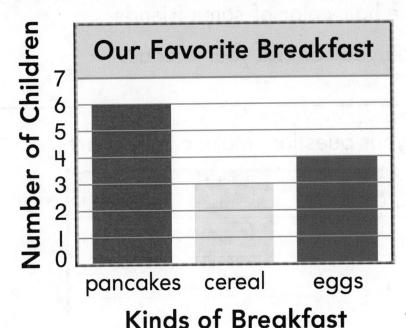

4. How many children chose pancakes?

○ 7
○ 4
○ 6

5. How many children chose eggs?

○ 6
○ 4
○ 3

6. How many fewer children chose cereal than pancakes?

○ 3
○ 2
○ 4

✓ Unit 5 Assessment

Vocabulary

1. Circle the **picture graph**. (p. 660)

2. Use the picture graph to complete the **bar graph**. (p. 672)

Our Favorite Juice

Each 🧍 stands for 1 child.

Kinds of Juice

Our Favorite Juice

0 1 2 3 4 5 6 7
Number of Children

Concepts and Skills

Use the graphs above to answer the questions. ◆ TEKS 1.8.C

3. Use the picture graph to write a question.

_____

4. Use the bar graph to write a question.

_____

5. How many more children chose
   🍎 than 🍊?

   _____ more children

6. Which juice did more children
   choose? Circle it.

Choose the correct answer.

7. How many children chose soccer? ▼ TEKS 1.8.A

Our Favorite Sport		Total
🥎 t-ball	|||	3
⚽ soccer	⊮ |	

○ 3
○ 6
○ 4

8. Which snack did the most children choose? ▼ TEKS 1.8.A

Our Favorite Snack		Total
🍌 banana	⊮	5
🥨 pretzel	|||	3
raisins	||	2

○

○

○

9. How many children chose ▭ RED ▭ ? ▼ TEKS 1.8.A

Color We Like						
▭ RED ▭ red	☿	☿	☿	☿	☿	
▭ BLUE ▭ blue	☿	☿	☿	☿	☿	☿

Each ☿ stands for 1 child.

○ 6 children

○ 3 children

○ 5 children

Choose the correct answer.

10. How many more days this month had 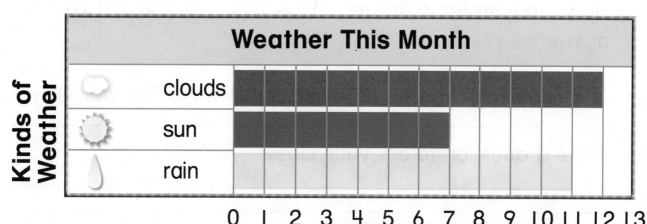 than ☀ ? ⬦ TEKS 1.8.C

Weather This Month

Kinds of Weather		
☁	clouds	
☀	sun	
💧	rain	

0 1 2 3 4 5 6 7 8 9 10 11 12 13
Number of Days

○ 5 more days   ○ 4 more days   ○ 11 more days

11. Sam makes a tally chart to show how many cars and trucks he has. Which group of tally marks shows how many cars Sam has? ⬦ TEKS 1.8.C

Sam's Cars and Trucks		Total
🚗 cars		8
🛻 trucks	‖‖‖ I	6

○ ‖‖‖ III   ○ ‖‖‖ I   ○ ‖‖‖ IIII

Choose the correct answer.

12. Use the T-chart about children that do wear glasses or do not wear glasses to answer the question. ➤ TEKS 1.8.A

yes	no
III	LHI III

How many fewer children answered yes than no?

○ 8 fewer children | ○ 3 fewer children | ○ 5 fewer children

13. Write a question to ask your class.

_____

- -

_____

- Ask 10 children your question.
- Record the information in a T-chart or a tally chart.
- Show the same information in a picture graph or a bar graph.

Use numbers, pictures, or words to tell which thing is the favorite. Justify. Explain why your answer is reasonable. ➤ TEKS 1.8.A, 1.8.B, 1.8.C

- What information am I given?
- What is my plan or strategy?
- How can I solve?
- How can I check my answer?

Personal Financial Literacy

Show What You Know ✓

Check your understanding of important skills.

Name _____

Count Forward

Write the numbers to complete counting forward.

1. 9, 10, 11, ____, 13, 14, 15

2. ____, 36, 37, 38, 39, 40, ____

Count and Write Numbers to 10

How many objects are in each set?

3.

____ butterflies

4.

____ cat

5.

____ leaves

Add in Any Order

Use ▣▪ ▣▪ to add. Color to match.
Write each sum.

6.

1 + 4 = ____

7.

4 + 1 = ____

 FAMILY NOTE: This page checks your child's understanding of important skills needed for success in Unit 6.

 GO DIGITAL Assessment Options: Soar to Success Math

Vocabulary Builder

Words

bike
clothes
food
house
radio
toys

Visualize It

Sort the words from the box.

Wants

_____

_____

_____

Needs

_____

_____

_____

Understand Vocabulary

Count. Write the total value.

1.   _____

2.   _____

3.   _____

Jenny Hen's Penny Bakery

written by Tim Johnson

illustrated by Diane Greenseid

This Take-Home Book belongs to

_____

Reading and Writing Math

This take-home book will help you review coins.

MATHEMATICAL PROCESSES 1.1.A, 1.1.F

Jenny Hen, also known as Little Red,
runs a bakery and sells bread.
She also sells cakes and pies,
and pizzas too, in every size!

Duck comes in. He's first to buy.
He's come to get an apple pie.
"Five pennies for the pie," says Jenny.
"Oh, dear Hen, I haven't any."

"Oh me, oh my, this is a pickle.
I have no pennies, just a nickel!"
Jenny smiles, "Then you're in luck.
A nickel's worth five pennies, Duck!"

Happy he can buy his pie,
Duck lets out a great big sigh.
He leaves the store and in comes Ted,
a tabby cat, to buy some bread.

"Wheat or white?" asks Jenny.
"Either one will cost ten pennies."

Says Ted, "Oh woe is me, and
what a crime. I haven't pennies,
just this dime." Jenny smiles,
and says, "Oh, please don't fret!
A dime's worth ten pennies!
So you're all set!"

If you ran a bakery, what would you sell? How much would you charge for your bakery items? Draw pictures to show your ideas.

Write about the Math

Write Math ▸ Look at the picture. Draw and write your own story about the bakery. Tell what you can buy and how much it costs.

Vocabulary Review
penny
nickel
dime

_____
_ _ _ _ _ _ _ _ _ _ _ _ _ _ _ _ _ _
_____
_____
_ _ _ _ _ _ _ _ _ _ _ _ _ _ _ _ _ _
_____
_ _ _ _ _ _ _ _ _ _ _ _ _ _ _ _ _ _
_____
_ _ _ _ _ _ _ _ _ _ _ _ _ _ _ _ _ _
_____

What Is It Worth?

Jenny Hen sells pie for 5¢ at her bakery.

1. What coin has a value of 5¢?

_____

2. Duck finds a nickel. Now he has 2 nickels. How many pies can he buy?

_____ pies

3. What coin has the same value as 2 nickels?

_____

4. Bread costs 10¢ at the bakery. You have 1 nickel and 4 pennies. Can you buy the bread? Explain.

_____

_____

_____

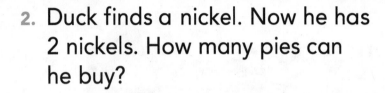 Write a story about buying cookies at the bakery. Tell how much each cookie costs. Tell how much it costs for more than 1 cookie.

_____

_____

_____

Name _____

20.1 Earn Money

? Essential Question

How and why do people earn income?

Explore Real World

Hands On

Use coins. Show the amount in different ways. Draw one way.

Math Talk
Mathematical Processes

How many nickels would Jake trade for 2 quarters? **Explain.**

FOR THE TEACHER • Read the following problem. Jake has two quarters. He wants to trade the quarters for other coins. What are some ways he can trade?

Emma **earns** 10¢ each time she walks the dog. What does Emma earn for walking the dog 5 times?

Money earned is **income.**

10¢ ___ ___ ___ ___

Emma earns 50¢.

Share and Show

Use coins. Draw and label the coins. Write the total income earned.

1. Hudson earns 5¢ each time he feeds the dog. What does Hudson earn for feeding the dog 6 times?

_____

✓2. In his store, Mr. Hudson fixes toys for 25¢. What does he earn for fixing 3 toys?

_____

Problem Solving

Use coins. Draw and label the coins.
Write the total income earned.

3. Paulo earns 10¢ each time he makes his bed. What does Paulo earn for making his bed 7 times?

_____

4. **H.O.T.** Andi earns 21¢ each time she puts her toys away. What does Andi earn for putting her toys away 4 times?

_____

5. **H.O.T.** Ray earns 16¢ each day he rakes leaves. He needs about 70¢ to buy a toy. Circle the best estimate for when he will have enough income to buy the toy.

| about 2 days | about 5 days | about 20 days |

Daily Assessment Task

Choose the correct answer. You may use coins.

6. **Apply** Lisa takes care of her aunt's cat for 4 days. She earns 10¢ a day. How much money does Lisa earn?

   ○ 40¢   ○ 4¢   ○ 14¢

7. Ana makes bracelets. She sells them at a yard sale for 5¢ each. She sells 5 bracelets. How much money does Ana earn?

   ○ 55¢   ○ 25¢   ○ 10¢

8. **Multi-Step** Morgan works 3 hours. Morgan is paid 10¢ for each hour. Taylor works 4 hours. Taylor is paid 5¢ for each hour. How much money do Morgan and Taylor earn together?

   ○ 15¢   ○ 70¢   ○ 50¢

9. ⭐ **TEXAS Test Prep** Casey makes cookies to sell at the fair. He earns 10¢ for each cookie he sells. What does Casey earn for selling 9 cookies?

   ○ 91¢   ○ 19¢   ○ 90¢

TEKS Personal Financial Literacy—1.9.A
Also 1.4.C
MATHEMATICAL PROCESSES 1.1.A, 1.1.C

20.1 Earn Money

Use coins. Draw and label the coins.
Write the total income earned.

1. Marty earns 11¢ each time he dries the
   dishes. What does Marty earn for drying
   the dishes 5 times?

   _____

Problem Solving (Real World)

Use coins. Draw and label the coins.

2. Gene earns 10¢ each time he walks the
   dog. He says that if he walks the dog
   4 times, his total income will be the same
   value as 2 quarters. Is he right? Explain.

   _____

   _____

   _____

   _____

Lesson Check

Choose the correct answer.

3. Mia takes care of the fish at the pet store for 3 days. She earns 25¢ a day. How much money does Mia earn?

   ○ 50¢   ○ 95¢   ○ 75¢

4. Denny makes lemonade. He sells glasses of lemonade for 10¢ each. He sells 8 glasses. How much money does Denny earn?

   ○ 18¢   ○ 80¢   ○ 70¢

5. Billy is paid 18¢ each time he cleans his room. He needs 45¢ for a snack. About how many times does he need to clean his room to be able to buy the snack?

   ○ about 9 times
   ○ about 7 times
   ○ about 3 times

TEKS **Personal Financial Literacy—1.9.B**
Also 1.4.C
MATHEMATICAL PROCESSES
1.1.A, 1.1.C, 1.1.D

20.2 Wants and Needs

? Essential Question

How are wants and needs different?

 Explore Real World   Hands On

Draw to show goods the family might purchase.

Draw to show a service the family might purchase.

Math Talk
Mathematical Processes

How are goods and services alike? How are they different?

 FOR THE TEACHER • Read the following problem. Samantha's family uses the money they earn to purchase goods and services. What are some ways they might use their income? Draw to show your answers.

Model and Draw

Kent uses his income first to buy things he **needs**.
If he has money left, he buys things he **wants**.

Needs	Wants

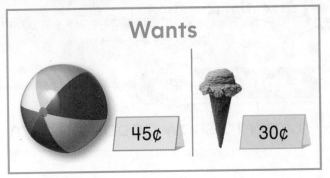

Find the total cost of Kent's needs. _____ + _____ = _____

Share and Show

MATH BOARD

Carla is going to eat breakfast.

☑1. Circle two things Carla needs. Cross out
one thing that is a want. Find the total
cost of the things she needs. Use coins.

_____ + _____ = _____

☑2. Describe how something you **want** is different
from something you **need**.

Name _____

3. **H.O.T.** Sophia is going to eat lunch. Circle two things Sophia needs. Cross out one thing that is a want. Find the total cost of the things she needs. Use coins.

 41¢  Chocolate Bar 47¢  18¢

_____ + _____ = _____

4. **H.O.T.** **Multi-Step** Circle **need** or **want** for these services. Explain your choice.

eat dinner at a restaurant

_____   **need**

_____   **want**

have someone fix a broken window

_____   **need**

_____   **want**

have someone wash your pet dog

_____   **need**

_____   **want**

Choose the correct answer. You may use coins.

5.  20¢ |  30¢ | 60¢

Apply Chloe is getting dressed for school. What is the total cost of the two things above that she might need?

- ○ 90¢
- ○ 80¢
- ○ 50¢

6. Draw or write to show something else Chloe might need when she is getting dressed for school. Tell why it is a need.

7. Draw or write to show something Chloe might want, but does not need, when she is getting dressed for school. Tell why it is a want.

8. ⭐ **TEXAS Test Prep**

 40¢ | 30¢ | 9¢

Nia is making a salad. What is the total cost of the two things above that she might need for the salad?

- ○ 70¢
- ○ 49¢
- ○ 39¢

TEKS Personal Financial Literacy—1.9.B
Also 1.4.C

MATHEMATICAL PROCESSES 1.1.A, 1.1.C, 1.1.D

Name _____

20.2 Wants and Needs

1. Madison is going to eat breakfast. Circle two things Madison needs. Cross out one thing that is a want. Find the total cost of the things she needs. Use coins.

 40¢   22¢    24¢

_____ + _____ = _____

Problem Solving Real World

2. Draw or write to show something Madison might want, but does not need, when she is eating breakfast. Tell why it is a want.

Choose the correct answer. You may use coins.

3.

 40¢   30¢   25¢

Eve is going on a hike. What is the total cost of the two things above that she might need?

○ 70¢   ○ 65¢   ○ 55¢

4.

 7¢    30¢    20¢

Andy is making blueberry muffins. What is the total cost of the two things above that he needs?

○ 50¢   ○ 37¢   ○ 57¢

5. Draw or write to show a service people need. Tell why it is a need. Then draw or write to show a service people want. Tell why it is a want.

Need	Want

TEKS Personal Financial Literacy—1.9.C
Also 1.3.D, 1.4.C, 1.5.G
MATHEMATICAL PROCESSES
1.1.A, 1.1.C, 1.1.F

20.3 Spend and Save

 Essential Question

Why is it important to know the difference between saving money and spending money?

Explore Real World

Hands On

Which items might you need for breakfast?
Which items do you not need?

Math Talk
Mathematical Processes

How do you decide what food you need to buy for breakfast?

 FOR THE TEACHER • Suppose you are grocery shopping for items you need for breakfast. Circle the items you might need. Cross out the items you do not need. Draw one more item you might need.

Model and Draw

Jon earns 10¢ each week for three weeks.
He can **save** the money or **spend** the money.

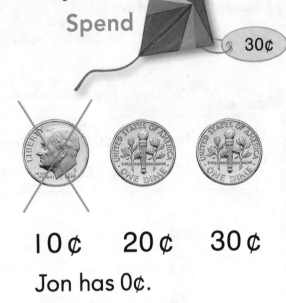

Save	Spend

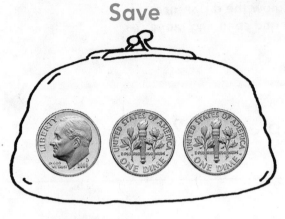

10¢ _____ _____

Jon has 30¢.

10¢   20¢   30¢

Jon has 0¢.

> What does save mean?

> What does spend mean?

Share and Show

MATH BOARD

Use coins. Draw and label the coins you
use. Write the answer.

✓1. Erica saves 12¢ each week for four
weeks. How much money does
Erica save?

_____

✓2. David has 15¢. He spends 8¢ to buy a
toy airplane. How much money does
David have left?

_____

Name _____

Use coins. Draw and label the coins you use. Write the answer.

3. Sam saves 15¢ each week for three weeks. How much money does Sam save?

_____

4. Jodi has 16¢. She spends 7¢ to buy a gift for her sister. How much money does Jodi have left?

_____

5.  **Multi-Step** Maya saves 20¢ on Monday, 40¢ on Tuesday, and 10¢ on Wednesday. How much money does Maya save?

_____

Choose the correct answer. Draw to show what you did to solve the problem. You may use coins.

6. Amy spends 20¢ each week for three weeks. How much money does Amy spend?

   ○ 40¢   ○ 60¢   ○ 23¢

7. **Apply** Reid saves 11¢ each week for 6 weeks. How much money does Reid save?

   ○ 61¢   ○ 17¢   ○ 66¢

8. Brian has 12¢. He spends 7¢ to buy a pencil. How much money does Brian have left?

   ○ 5¢   ○ 19¢   ○ 10¢

9. ⭐ **TEXAS Test Prep** Chris has 50¢. He puts 3 dimes in his bank, and uses the rest to buy a baseball. How much does Chris spend on the baseball?

   ○ 30¢   ○ 80¢   ○ 20¢

TEKS Personal Financial Literacy—1.9.C
Also 1.3.D, 1.4.C, 1.5.G
MATHEMATICAL PROCESSES 1.1.A, 1.1.C, 1.1.F

Name _____

20.3 Spend and Save

Use coins. Draw and label the coins
you use. Write the answer.

1. Devon saves 11¢ each week for five weeks.
   How much money does Devon save?

   _____

Problem Solving Real World

Use coins. Draw and label the coins you use.
Write the answer.

2. Maxi has 18¢. She spends 9¢ to buy
   a horn for her bike. How much money
   does Maxi have left?

   _____

3. **Multi-Step** Brian saves 50¢ on Monday and
   30¢ on Tuesday. Then he spends 20¢ to rent a
   movie. How much money does Brian have left?

   _____

Choose the correct answer. You may use coins.

4. Nan spends 10¢ each day for five days. How much money does Nan spend?

   ○ 25¢   ○ 50¢   ○ 15¢

5. Ric saves 12¢ each week for 3 weeks. How much money does Ric save?

   ○ 36¢   ○ 33¢   ○ 15¢

6. Abby has 16¢. She spends 9¢ to buy a card. How much money does Abby have left?

   ○ 7¢   ○ 9¢   ○ 25¢

7. Maria has 70¢. She spends 20¢ for hair ribbons and saves the rest. How much money does Maria save?

   ○ 95¢   ○ 45¢   ○ 50¢

20.4 Give to Charity

TEKS Personal Financial Literacy—1.9.D
Also 1.4.A, 1.4.B, 1.4.C
MATHEMATICAL PROCESSES
1.1.A, 1.1.C

? Essential Question

What are some ways that you can share with others?

Explore

Draw to show a way you can share with others.

 FOR THE TEACHER • Have children discuss ways they can help and share with others. Then have them draw to show one way they share.

Math Talk
Mathematical Processes
What can you do to share with others?

Model and Draw

Rachel's family shares some of the money they earn with others. Rachel puts some coins to share in a jar.

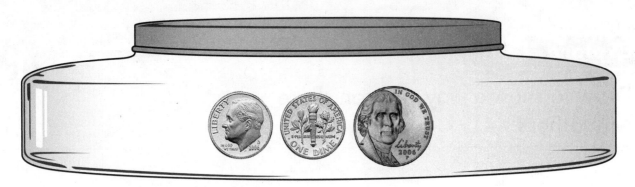

Giving to or sharing with others in need is **charity**.

What is the total value of the coins? _____

Share and Show

Answer the question. You may use coins.

1. Cindi puts these coins in the sharing jar. What is the total value of these coins?

_____

2. Ava puts 1 quarter, 4 dimes, and 5 pennies in the sharing jar. What is the total value of these coins? Draw and label the coins you use.

_____

Problem Solving

Answer the question. You may use coins.

3. Nina puts these coins in the sharing jar. What is the total value of these coins?

_____

4. Liz puts 3 quarters, I dime, and I nickel in the sharing jar. What is the total value of these coins?

_____

5. **H.O.T.** Ross has I quarter, 3 dimes, and 2 pennies. He puts one coin in the sharing jar. The total value of the coins he has left is 47¢. Which coin did Ross put in the jar?

_____

6. **H.O.T.** **Multi-Step** Glenn has 3 quarters and 2 dimes. He puts I quarter and I dime in the sharing jar. What is the total value of the coins he has left?

_____

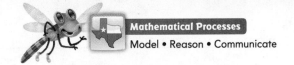
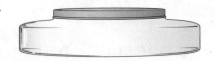
Daily Assessment Task

Choose the correct answer.
You may use coins.

7. Mel puts these coins in the sharing jar.
   What is the total value of these coins?

   ○ 40¢   ○ 25¢   ○ 30¢

8. **Apply** Raul puts 1 quarter, 2 nickels,
   and 3 pennies in the sharing jar. What
   is the total value of these coins?

   ○ 38¢   ○ 48¢   ○ 30¢

9. **Multi-Step** Lola has 3 quarters, 1 nickel,
   and 1 penny. She puts 1 quarter in the
   sharing jar. What is the total value of the
   coins Lola has left?

   ○ 81¢   ○ 86¢   ○ 56¢

10. ⭐ **TEXAS Test Prep** Adan puts 4 dimes in
    the sharing jar on Monday. He puts 2 dimes
    and 1 nickel in the jar on Tuesday. What
    is the total value of the coins Adan puts
    in the jar?

    ○ 70¢   ○ 75¢   ○ 65¢

Name _____

20.4 Give to Charity

Answer the question. You may use coins.

1. Dee puts these coins in the sharing jar. What is the total value of these coins?

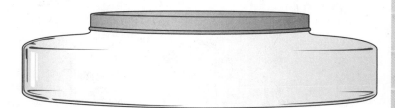

_____

2. Sherri puts 2 quarters, 1 dime, and 2 pennies in the sharing jar. What is the total value of these coins?

_____

Problem Solving

Answer the question. You may use coins.

3. **Multi-Step** Marissa has 2 quarters and 3 dimes. She puts 1 quarter and 2 dimes in the sharing jar. What is the total value of the coins she has left?

_____

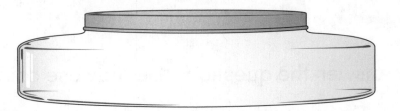
Choose the correct answer. You may use coins.

4. Vicki puts these coins in the sharing jar. What is the total value of these coins?

○ 85¢   ○ 80¢   ○ 75¢

5. Sean puts 3 dimes, 3 nickels, and 6 pennies in the sharing jar. What is the total value of these coins?

○ 51¢   ○ 66¢   ○ 61¢

6. Ali puts I quarter in the sharing jar on Monday. She puts 3 dimes and 2 pennies in the jar on Tuesday. What is the total value of the coins Ali puts in the jar?

○ 55¢   ○ 57¢   ○ 52¢

7. **Multi-Step** Jimmy has I quarter, 3 nickels, and 4 pennies. He puts 3 nickels and 2 pennies in the sharing jar. What is the total value of the coins Jimmy has left?

○ 25¢   ○ 44¢   ○ 27¢

Unit 6 Assessment

Vocabulary

Use the words in the box to complete the sentences. (pp. 718, 724, 736)

| charity |
| spend |
| income |
| needs |

1. Money you earn when you work is _____.

2. Giving to others in need is _____.

3. Things that are necessary are _____.

Concepts and Skills

4. Raul's family uses some of their income to buy services. Draw to show a service they might need and a service they might want. ↪ TEKS 1.9.B

5. Piper has 60¢. She buys a ball for 40¢ and a kite with the rest of her money.
   Lexi has 60¢. She puts 35¢ in her bear bank and the rest in her turtle bank. ↪ TEKS 1.9.C

   Which child saved her money? _____

   Which child spent her money? _____

   Write or draw to explain how you know.

Choose the correct answer.
You may use coins.

6. Carter earns 13¢ each time he feeds the cat.
What is Carter's income if he feeds the cat
3 times? TEKS 1.9.A

   ○ 43¢   ○ 39¢   ○ 16¢

---

7. Darien has 18¢. He spends 9¢ to buy a book.
How much money does Darien have left? TEKS 1.9.C

   ○ 9¢   ○ 27¢   ○ 11¢

8.

7¢   15¢   50¢

Grant is getting dressed for school. What is
the total cost of the two things above that
he might need? TEKS 1.9.B

   ○ 22¢   ○ 65¢   ○ 57¢

Choose the correct answer. You may use coins.

9. Lola puts these coins in the sharing jar.
   What is the total value of these coins? 🔻 TEKS 1.9.D

○ 55¢   ○ 90¢   ○ 80¢

---

10. Emily puts 1 quarter, 3 dimes, and 1 nickel
    in the sharing jar. What is the total value
    of these coins? 🔻 TEKS 1.9.D

○ 60¢   ○ 45¢   ○ 65¢

---

11. Kari earns 15¢ each time she makes her bed.
    What is Kari's income if she makes her
    bed 5 times? 🔻 TEKS 1.9.A

○ 50¢   ○ 75¢   ○ 20¢

Choose the correct answer.
You may use coins.

12. Sam saves 12¢ each week for four weeks. How much money does Sam save? ◆ TEKS 1.9.C

○ 40¢   ○ 48¢   ○ 16¢

13. Betsy earns 6 coins for walking the dog. Only one coin is a quarter.

What coins could Betsy have? What is the total value?

Use numbers, pictures, or words to show your work.
Justify. Explain why your answer is reasonable. ◆ TEKS 1.9.A

• What information am I given?
• What is my plan or strategy?
• How can I solve?
• How can I check my answer?

Picture Glossary

add sumar

3 + 2 = 5

addend sumando

1 + 3 = 4

addend

addition sentence oración de suma

2 + 1 = 3 is an **addition sentence.**

bar graph gráfica de barras

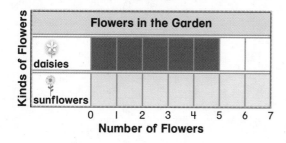

Flowers in the Garden

Kinds of Flowers

daisies

sunflowers

0 1 2 3 4 5 6 7
Number of Flowers

cent(¢) centavo

A penny is 1 **cent.**

1¢

charity caridad

Giving to others in need is **charity.**

circle círculo

compare comparar

Subtract to **compare** groups.

5 − 1 = 4

There are more ⬤.

cone cono

---

count back contar hacia atrás

$8 - 1 = 7$

Start at 8.

Count back 1.

You are on 7.

---

count on contar hacia adelante

$4 + 2 = 6$

Say 4.

Count on 2.

5, 6

cube cubo

---

curved surface superficie curva

Some three-dimensional shapes have a **curved surface.**

---

cylinder cilindro

difference diferencia

$$4 - 3 = 1$$

The **difference** is 1.

---

digit dígito

13 is a two-**digit** number.

The 1 in 13 means 1 ten.

The 3 in 13 means 3 ones.

---

dime moneda de 10¢

 or   10¢
10 cents

doubles dobles

$$5 + 5 = 10$$

---

doubles minus one dobles
menos uno

$$5 + 5 = 10, \text{ so } 5 + 4 = 9$$

---

doubles plus one dobles
más uno

$$5 + 5 = 10, \text{ so } 5 + 6 = 11$$

earn ganar

You **earn** money when you work.

edge arista

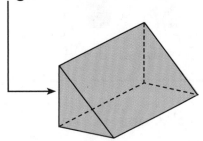

equal parts partes iguales

These show **equal parts**, or equal shares.

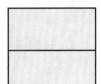

equal shares porciones iguales

These show equal parts, or **equal shares**.

face cara

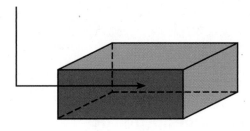

fewer menos

3 **fewer**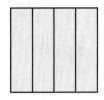

flat surface superficie plana

Some three-dimensional shapes have only **flat surfaces**.

fourth of cuarto de

A **fourth of** this shape is shaded.

fourths cuartos

 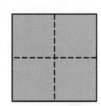

I whole   4 **fourths**, or 4 quarters

greatest el mayor

58   51   46

greatest

half hour media hora

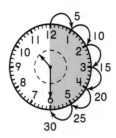

A **half hour** has 30 minutes.

half of mitad de

Half of this shape is shaded.

halves mitades

 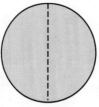

I whole   2 **halves**

hexagon hexágono

hour hora

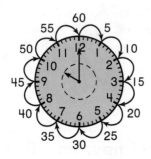

An **hour** has 60 minutes.

---

hour hand horario

hour hand →

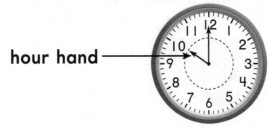

---

hundred centena

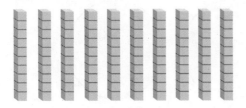

10 tens is the same
as 1 **hundred**.

---

income ingreso

Money you get when you
work is **income**.

---

is equal to (=) es igual a

2 plus 1 **is equal to** 3.

$$2 + 1 = 3$$

---

is greater than (>) es mayor
que

35 is **greater than** 27.

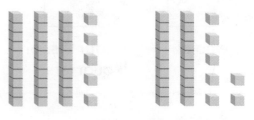

$$35 > 27$$

is less than (<) es menor que

43 is **less than** 49.

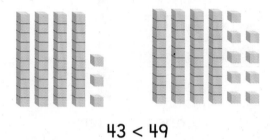

43 < 49

---

least el menor

46   51   58

least

---

length longitud

You can use string to measure the **length** of the pencil box.

make a ten formar una decena

Move 2 counters into the ten frame. **Make a ten.**

$$\begin{array}{r} 8 \\ + 4 \\ \hline 12 \end{array}$$

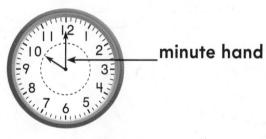

---

minus (−) menos

4 **minus** 3 is equal to 1.

$4 - 3 = 1$

---

minute hand minutero

← **minute hand**

---

minutes minutos

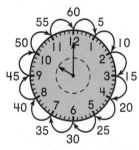

An hour has 60 **minutes**.

more más

$5 - 1 = 4$

There are **more** .

---

needs necesidades

Things that are necessary are **needs**.

---

nickel moneda de 5¢

 or

5¢
5 cents

---

ones unidades

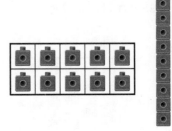

10 **ones** = 1 ten

---

order orden

You can change the **order** of the addends.

$1 + 3 = 4$ $3 + 1 = 4$

---

penny moneda de 1¢

 or

1¢
1 cent

---

picture graph gráfica de dibujos

Our Favorite Activity at the Fair							
animals	𝖞	𝖞	𝖞	𝖞	𝖞		
rides	𝖞	𝖞	𝖞	𝖞	𝖞	𝖞	𝖞

Each 𝖞 stands for 1 child.

plus (+) más

2 **plus** I is equal to 3.

$$2 + 1 = 3$$

---

quarter moneda de 25¢

 or

25¢
25 **cents**

---

quarter of cuarta parte de

A **quarter of** this shape
is shaded.

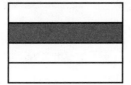

quarters cuartas partes

I whole   4 fourths,
or 4 **quarters**

---

rectangle rectángulo

A square is a
special kind of
rectangle.

---

rectangular prism prisma
rectangular

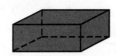

A cube is a special
kind of rectangular
prism.

related facts operaciones relacionadas

$4 + 5 = 9$

$9 - 5 = 4$

$5 + 4 = 9$

$9 - 4 = 5$

rhombus rombo

save ahorrar

You **save** money when you keep it.

shortest el más corto

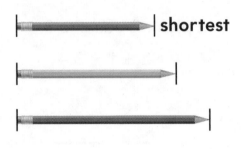

shortest

side lado

side

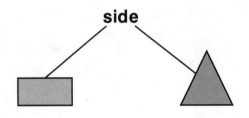

skip count contar salteado

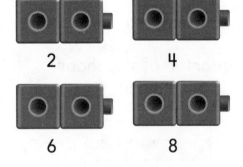

2

4

6

8

spend gastar

You **spend** money when you use it to buy things.

sphere esfera

square cuadrado

subtract restar

Subtract to find out how many.

subtraction sentence
oración de resta

$4 - 3 = 1$ is a **subtraction sentence.**

sum suma o total

2 **plus** 1 is equal to 3.

The **sum** is 3.

T-chart Gráfica de T

soccer	swimming
卌 II	III

tally chart tabla de conteo

Boys and Girls in Our Class		Total
boys	卌 IIII	9
girls	卌 I	6

tally mark marca de conteo

IIII

Each tally mark **|** stands for 1.
IIII stands for 5.

---

ten decena

10 ones = 1 **ten**

---

triangle triángulo

triangular prism prisma triangular

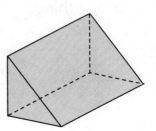

---

unequal parts partes desiguales

These show **unequal parts**, or unequal shares.

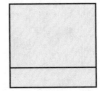 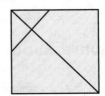

---

unequal shares porciones desiguales

These show unequal parts, or **unequal shares**.

 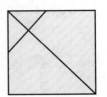

unit unidad

Each 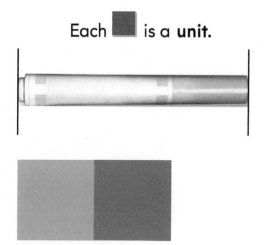 is a **unit**.

wants deseos

Things you wish for
are **wants**.

vertex vértice

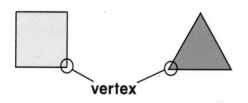

vertex

zero 0 cero

When you add **zero** to
any number, the sum
is that number.

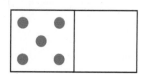

$$5 + 0 = 5$$